GREAT MILITARY LEADERS

Montezuma II

Elizabeth Schulz

Published in 2018 by Cavendish Square Publishing, LLC
243 5th Avenue, Suite 136, New York, NY 10016

Copyright © 2018 by Cavendish Square Publishing, LLC

First Edition

No part of this publication may be reproduced, stored in a retrieval system, or transmitted in any form or by any means—electronic, mechanical, photocopying, recording, or otherwise—without the prior permission of the copyright owner. Request for permission should be addressed to Permissions, Cavendish Square Publishing,
243 5th Avenue, Suite 136, New York, NY 10016.
Tel (877) 980-4450; fax (877) 980-4454.

Website: cavendishsq.com

This publication represents the opinions and views of the author based on his or her personal experience, knowledge, and research. The information in this book serves as a general guide only. The author and publisher have used their best efforts in preparing this book and disclaim liability rising directly or indirectly from the use and application of this book.

CPSIA Compliance Information: Batch #CS17CSQ

All websites were available and accurate when this book was sent to press.

Library of Congress Cataloging-in-Publication Data

Names: Schulz, Elizabeth, (Author), author.
Title: Montezuma II / Elizabeth Schulz.
Description: New York : Cavendish Square Publishing, 2018. |
Series: Greatmilitary leaders | Includes bibliographical references and index.
Identifiers: LCCN 2017006900 (print) | LCCN 2017008178 (ebook) |
ISBN 9781502627896 (library bound) | ISBN 9781502627902 (E-book)
Subjects: LCSH: Montezuma II, Emperor of Mexico, approximately 1480-1520--Juvenile literature. | Aztecs--Kings and rulers--Biography--Juvenile literature. | Mexico--History--Conquest, 1519-1540--Juvenile literature. | Aztecs--History--Juvenile literature.
Classification: LCC F1230.M6 S38 2018 (print) | LCC F1230.M6 (ebook) | DDC 972/.018092 [B] --dc23
LC record available at https://lccn.loc.gov/2017006900

Editorial Director: David McNamara
Editor: Molly Fox
Copy Editor: Rebecca Rohan
Associate Art Director: Amy Greenan
Designer: Jessica Nevins
Production Coordinator: Karol Szymczuk
Photo Research: J8 Media

The photographs in this book are used by permission and through the courtesy of: Cover De Agostini Picture Library/Getty Images; p. 4 Chronicle/Alamy Stock Photo; p. 8, 58 Photo Researchers/Alamy Stock Photo; p. 10 Madman2001/Wikimedia Commons/File:Lake Texcoco c 1519.png/CC BY SA 3.0; p. 14-15 DEA Picture Library/De Agostini/Getty Images; p. 17 Carver Mostardi/Alamy Stock Photo; 18, 22, 55, 78-79 North Wind Picture Archives; p.26 Byelikova Oksana/Shutterstock.com; p. 30 Universal History Archive/UIG/Getty Images; p. 32 Sasha Isachenko/Wikimedia Commons/File:Aztec calendar stone in National Museum of Anthropology, Mexico City.jpg/CC BY SA 3.0; p. 34 DEA/G. Dagli Orti/De Agostini/Getty Images; p. 37 Rafal Cichawa/Shutterstock.com; p. 41 ART Collection/Alamy Stock Photo; p. 50 World History Archive/Alamy Stock Photo; p. 52-53 Lebrecht Music and Arts Photo Library/Alamy Stock Photo; p. 57 Werner Forman/Universal Images Group/Getty Images; p. 62, 76 Bettmann/Getty Images; p. 66 Ann Ronan Pictures/Print Collector/Getty Images; p. 80 Yavidaxiu/Wikimedia Commons/File:Ruta de escape de los españoles hacia Tlaxcala.svg/CC BY SA 3.0; p. 83 Archiv Gerstenberg/ullstein bild/Getty Images; p. 85 Dorling Kindersley/Getty Images; p. 86-87 Spanish School/Getty Images; p. 98 Prisma/UIG/Getty Images; p. 101 Gary Francisco Keller, artwork created under supervision of Bernardino de Sahagún between 1540 and 1585/Wikimedia Commons/File:The Florentine Codex- Life in Mesoamerica III.tiff/CC BY SA 3.0; p. 102 Julie Alissi/J8 Media; p. 108 Private Collection/Archives Charmet/Bridgeman Images; p. 111 Alexmisu/Shutterstock.com.

Printed in the United States of America

TABLE OF CONTENTS

INTRODUCTION	5
CHAPTER 1 The Culture of the Aztec Empire	9
CHAPTER 2 The Life of Montezuma	31
CHAPTER 3 Waging War	51
CHAPTER 4 The Aftermath of La Noche Triste	77
CHAPTER 5 Myths, Legends, and Popular Culture	99
CHRONOLOGY	113
GLOSSARY	116
FURTHER INFORMATION	120
BIBLIOGRAPHY	122
INDEX	125
ABOUT THE AUTHOR	128

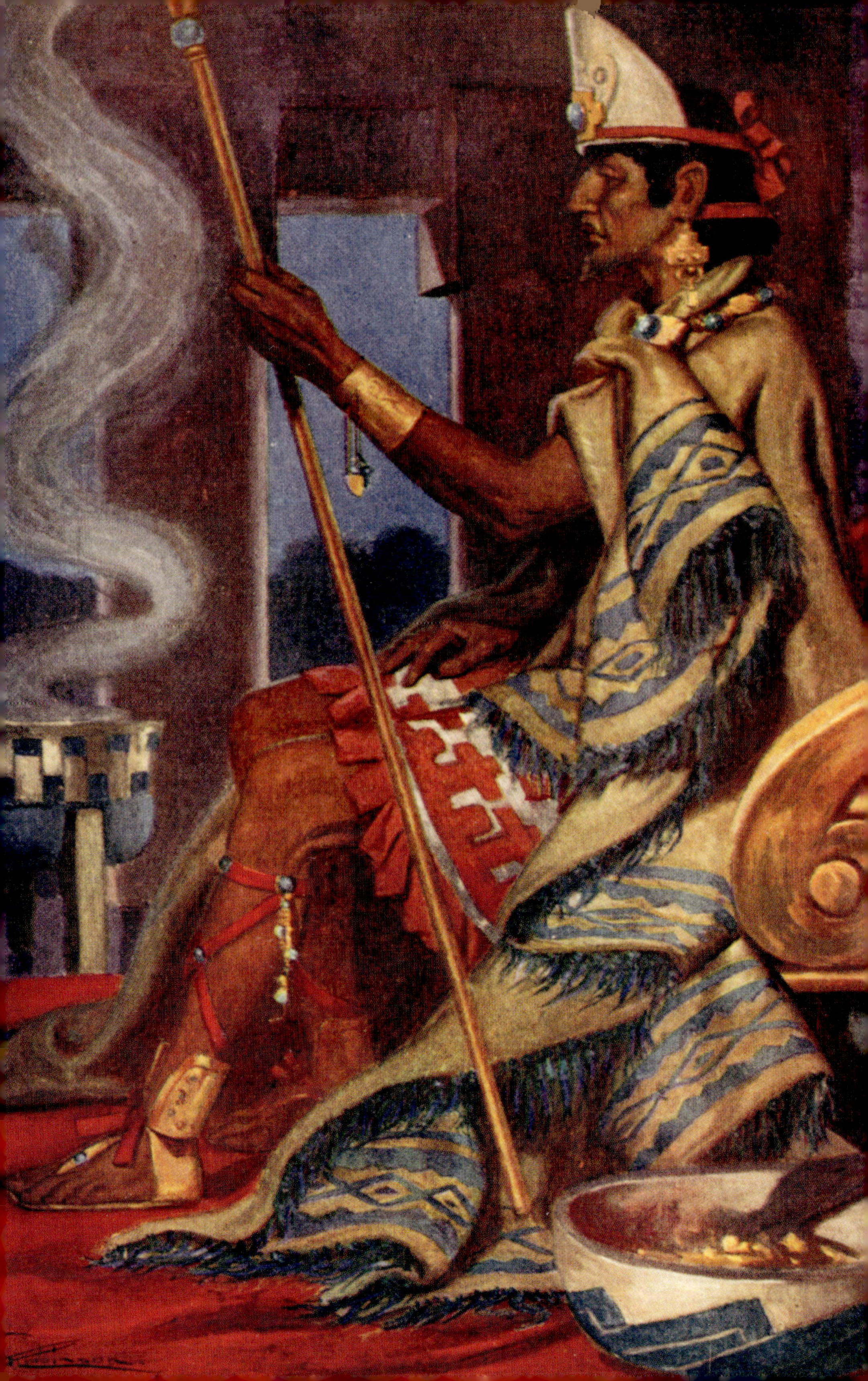

INTRODUCTION

The rise of the powerful Aztec empire is impressive. Rooted in nomadic origins, these wandering people traveled south from North America into the central valley of Mexico, eventually settling and founding their capital city. From this hub, they asserted their dominance over neighboring tribes across the valley. Within nearly two hundred years, the Aztecs ruled over a loosely knit empire extending from the Atlantic Ocean to the Pacific. By **subjugating** tribes, exacting "tax" from them in the form of **tribute**, exercising their military might, and imposing their patron god (and religion) onto conquered peoples, the Aztecs created a vast and powerful empire.

Montezuma II was the ninth, and some say last, Aztec emperor to rule. However, after his death, the empire did exist for one more year under the rule of two additional emperors. It would be fair to say that Montezuma II was the last *great* Aztec emperor. By the time he was elected emperor, Montezuma II had already proven himself to be a great military leader and high priest, attuned to the Aztec gods and their signs that foretold the future of the empire. Montezuma II was a well-rounded leader and a natural choice to take the helm of the ever-expanding powerful empire. Yet his tenure as emperor is overshadowed by the last year of his eighteen-year rule. His prior accomplishments seem to be diminished in comparison to the choices he made, and

Opposite: Montezuma sits on his throne in his palace within the Aztec capital of Tenochtitlán.

their outcomes, between 1519 and 1520, the year he encountered the Spanish **conquistadors**.

In this book, Montezuma II's story has been presented in a way to give the reader a sense of the complexities of the man as well as the conflicts he faced in his last year as emperor. It's easy, in contemporary times, to look back and be critical of him as a leader. Understanding him in a three-dimensional manner as he, and his people, faced the greatest challenge in Aztec history, is important.

When researching Montezuma II, there are discrepancies in historical information, source materials, names, dates, and general information. For example, the people now referred to as Aztec did not actually call themselves Aztec. Instead, they referred to themselves as **Mexica**. **Nahuatl** is the language spoken by the Aztecs and other members of the Nahua peoples. "Mexica" is the Nahuatl term for "people from Aztlan" or "place of the Mexica" (referring to the origin of the Nahua peoples). The sources used for this book include references to both "Aztecs" and "Mexica." For purposes of the book, the reader will see the term "Mexica" in quotes from source materials only. The rest of the time, the Aztecs will be referred to as "the Aztecs."

There are also different spellings of Montezuma II's name. Sometimes you will see it spelled as "Motecuhzoma" or "Moctezuma." In this book, his name is spelled "Montezuma." Research reveals that he was the second of two Aztec emperors named Montezuma. The first was named Moctezuma Ilhuicamina. The second, and great-grandson of the first, was born Motecuhzoma Xocoyotzin. He is often referred to as Moctezuma II to differentiate between the leaders. As the subject of this book, he will be referred to solely as Montezuma.

Slight discrepancies exist regarding some dates of events such as Montezuma's birth, news of the Spanish arrival off the coast of Mexico, the "night of sorrows," and Montezuma's death. Dates referred to in this book correlate with two of the main resources used and referenced: Cottie Arthur Burland's *Montezuma: Lord of the Aztecs* and Hugh Thomas's *Conquest: Cortes, Montezuma, and the Fall of Old Mexico*.

Lastly, primary source material about Montezuma, the Aztecs, their empire, and the Spanish conquest is limited, in the sense that original Aztec ancient texts and documents were burned by the Spanish. Once destroyed, the Spanish set about to reproduce Aztec documents (referred to as codices). Spanish friars, during the conversion of the pagan Aztecs to Christianity, worked with the conquered people, recreating texts to document Aztec daily life, beliefs, culture, and history. Of course, these reproductions have a Spanish flavor to them.

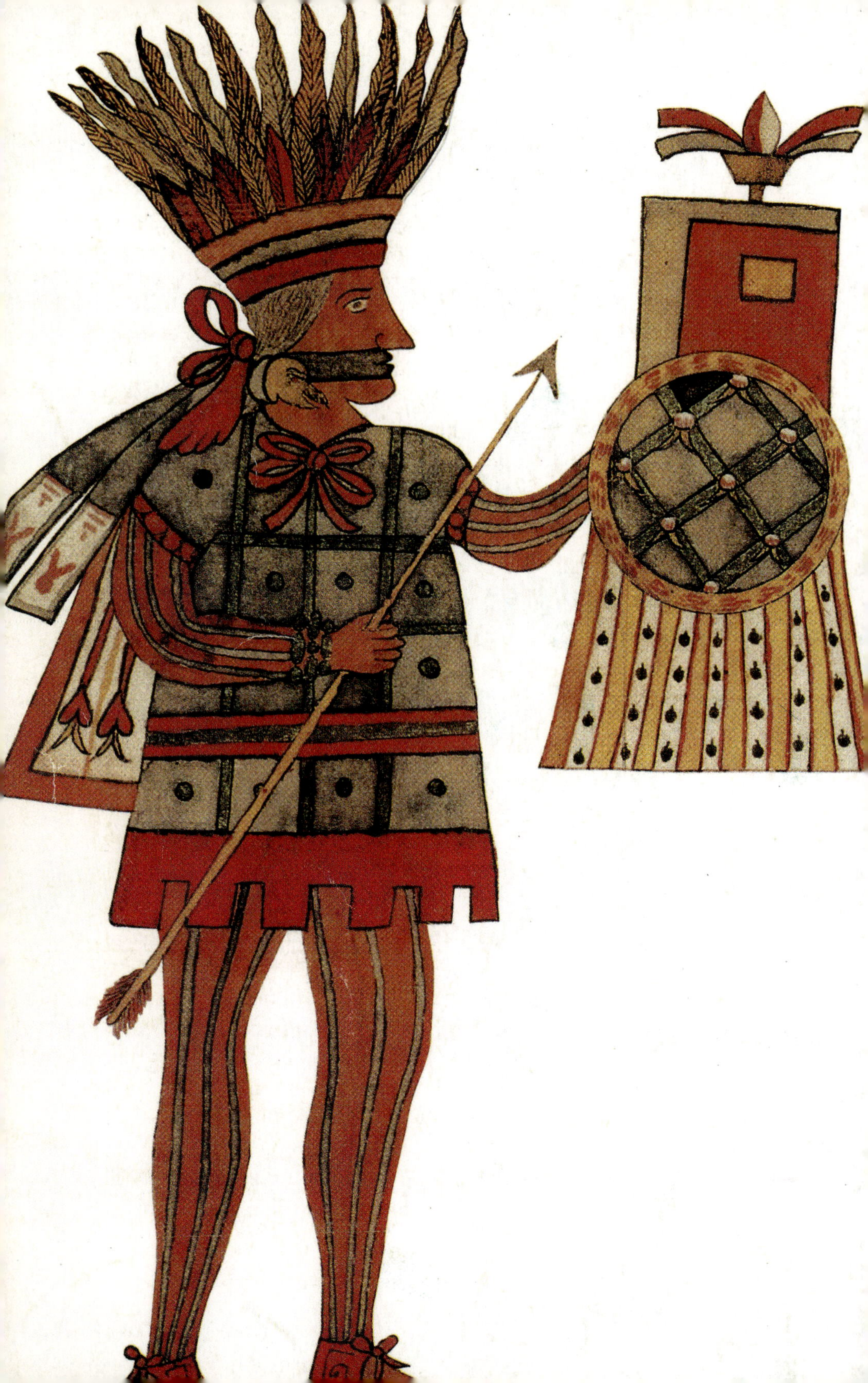

CHAPTER ONE

The Culture of the Aztec Empire

With origins as nomads, it is no wonder the Aztec culture was cobbled together, borrowing from other tribes encountered over the course of Aztec existence. Researchers believe the Aztecs were once hunters and gatherers who wore animal skins and lived in caves. It is thought that they "were descendants of the Asian people who arrived on the North American continent after crossing the Bering Strait during Earth's last Ice Age and migrating south, following the mammoth herds."

Nahuatl was the language spoken by the Aztecs. This language is from one of the largest Native American linguistic families, thought to have originated in what is now the southwestern United States. The original speakers of this language are thought to have reached central Mexico around 400 CE to 500 CE. The Aztecs were some of the last Nahuatl speakers to have migrated to central Mexico from the north.

Opposite: This representation shows Huitzilopochtli, the patron god of the Aztecs, wearing a headdress made of hummingbird feathers.

Mexico Valley c. 1519

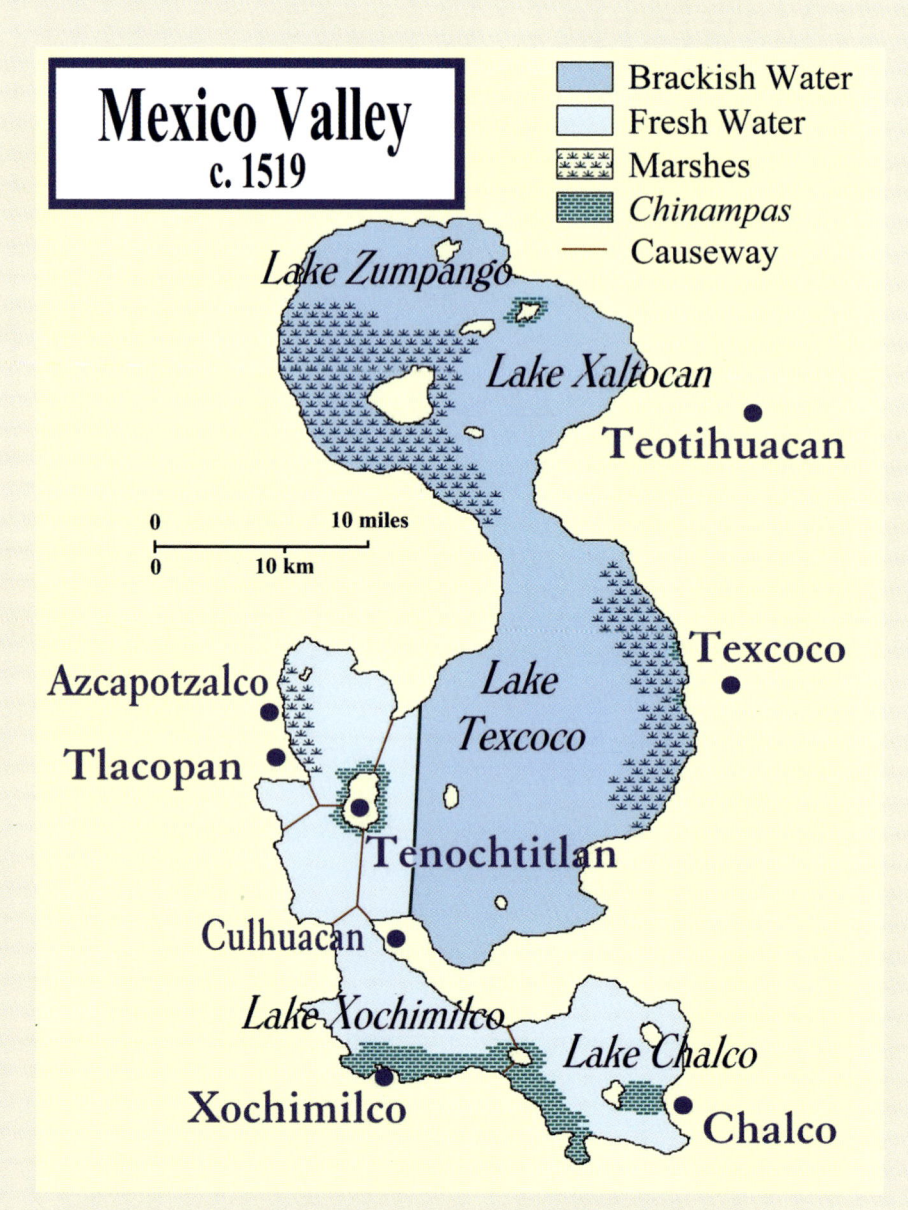

Legend:
- Brackish Water
- Fresh Water
- Marshes
- *Chinampas*
- Causeway

Locations:
- Lake Zumpango
- Lake Xaltocan
- Teotihuacan
- Azcapotzalco
- Tlacopan
- Texcoco
- Lake Texcoco
- Tenochtitlan
- Culhuacan
- Lake Xochimilco
- Lake Chalco
- Xochimilco
- Chalco

Scale: 0–10 miles / 0–10 km

The Aztecs dominated neighboring towns and tribes from their stronghold island city of Tenochtitlán, pictured in this map.

ORIGINS OF THE AZTECS

Nomadic in origin, the Mexica, or Aztecs, journeyed from the north down into **Anahuac** (Mexico). Legend says they heard strange whistling emanating from a carved stone representing the god **Huitzilopochtli** (Hummingbird-on-the-Left). The god promised them that if they remained faithful to him, they would conquer all of Mexico. Carrying the carved stone with them, the Aztecs wandered throughout central Mexico between 1100 and 1248 until they found a territory in which to settle. However, the Tepanecs, who occupied this land, quickly expelled them. The Aztecs continued their journey in the belief Huitzilopochtli would show them the way. By 1325, they at last saw the sign of their promised homeland: Huitzilopochtli appeared before them as a white eagle, holding a serpent, sitting on a prickly pear cactus that sprang from a rock. Their days of wandering were over.

Once settled, the Aztecs asserted their tribal identity and established a very dominant culture. They expanded their territory and subjugated conquered tribes in the process, by imposing their military might and justifying their actions with religion; more specifically, insisting their god Huitzilopochtli replace all other gods as the supreme deity for all conquered peoples. The Aztecs were faithful to Huitzilopochtli. In exchange, he offered protection and Aztec domination. The empire grew, expanding across Mexico over the course of nearly two hundred years.

Origins of Aztec Culture

By the time the Aztecs arrived in the valley of central Mexico, the land was crowded with competing Nahua tribes jockeying for dominance. Eventually splitting off from these tribes, the Aztecs continued to journey south in search of their homeland as promised to them by their god Huitzilopochtli. By 1325, they had found and settled in the place from which their powerful empire grew. Aztec culture is rooted in this journey and subsequent settlement; it's where their story really begins. Historian Mathilde Helly relays the Aztec journey story in this way:

> According to legend, it was an oracle that prompted their move and sealed their **fate**: Huitzilopochtli (Hummingbird-on-the-left, god of war and the noonday sun, supreme god of the Aztecs) was at once man, god, and sorcerer. He had the power to change himself into an eagle or a hummingbird and also had the power of speech. He ordered the Aztecs to set off and conquer the world and pointed the way to central Mexico.

Their centuries-long journey brought them to Lake Texcoco. In this lake was an island covered with rocks and prickly pear cactuses. A golden eagle sat perched on top of a cactus devouring a snake (the eagle and snake are seen in Mexico's national emblem today, appearing on their flag). The Aztecs knew that this was the sign from their god Huitzilopochtli to stop wandering and settle. On this island, they set about building a city that would become the hub from which they would dominate the land.

The Aztecs built their city and called it **Tenochtitlán** (meaning Cactus Rock). From this home base, the Aztecs began to establish a dominant religious and militaristic culture. They honored Huitzilopochtli, their god and protector, through religious rituals and military might, spreading their culture across newly conquered territories.

Aztec Life Before Montezuma's Time

Aztec life revolved around their gods and the worship of them. The Aztecs believed their world, or universe, was the fifth world created, the prior four having been destroyed. In the creation of this fifth world, and most importantly the sun, the gods had sacrificed their lives. Therefore, the Aztecs used human **sacrifice** as a way to honor these gods, and to prevent chaos and destruction of their world. Sacrifices maintained balance, ensuring the sun continued to move across the sky.

Huitzilopochtli, their supreme deity, was believed to be the sun. He was carried up into the middle of the sky (sunrise to noon time) by spirits of warriors who had died on the battlefield or on the sacrificial stone. He was then brought back down to Earth, at sunset, by the ghosts of women who had died in childbirth. This endless journey through the sky required regular nourishment—in the form of warm blood and beating hearts, for only blood and hearts ensured the survival of their universe. Without this, they thought, the world would be destroyed.

Very strict rules governed human sacrifice. The Aztecs did not sacrifice their fellow countrymen, strangers, or the sick. Sacrificial victims had to come from nearby nations. They also had to be healthy, with proven warrior abilities. Sacrifice was very sacred, and it was considered a great honor to be sacrificed. Blood sacrifices ensured Aztec civilization would continue. Some sacrifices, such as those involving vanquished enemies, included

14 Montezuma II

The Great Temple (*left*) stood in the middle of Tenochtitlán. Human sacrifices to the Aztec gods happened here.

The Culture of the Aztec Empire 15

cannibalism. Once the beating hearts were removed, Aztec priests would eat the flesh of the victims' arms and legs. Hearts were placed in a *chacmool* statue. This was a sculpture of a reclining figure holding a bowl. The hearts were presented as tribute to the gods in the chacmool. Sacrifice was integral to appease the wrath of their gods that threatened their existence.

Religion provided the Aztecs with meaning of both known and unknown phenomena. They routinely watched the sky for signs and **portents**, or warnings, from their gods. This helped them better understand their lives and their destinies. Believing the future would reveal itself through these signs, anything out of the ordinary was viewed as an **omen** of a coming event—often a disastrous event. The ***tonalpouhque***, or astrologer, specialized in reading the Aztec sacred texts, interpreting signs and numbers of their calendars. The Aztecs never attempted to contradict the signs in their world, accepting the interpretations of these astrologers.

Sacred texts, as well as government documentations, were written not with letters from an alphabet but rather using **glyphs**, or pictograms, that depicted what they wanted to convey. A glyph of a cactus meant a cactus, but if it was paired with other glyphs, it could mean a location or a more complex idea.

Though Huitzilopochtli was the supreme Aztec deity, another god figured centrally in Aztec culture: the god **Quetzalcoatl**. The Aztec creation myth describes two divinities (a lord and a lady) who form two halves of the same whole. They created themselves and lived in the Thirteenth Heaven. They had four sons: Xipe-Totec (Our Lord the Flayed), Tezcatlipoca (Smoking Mirror), Huitzilopochtli (Hummingbird-on-the-left), and Quetzalcoatl (Feathered Serpent).

The Aztecs believed Quetzalcoatl came to Earth in human form. At one time, this god had been a head of state, but forced

An Aztec ceremonial knife, intended for sacrifices, typically had decorative handles and blades of flint or obsidian.

The Culture of the Aztec Empire

Five priests hold victims down on the Great Temple altar for the high priest to sacrifice.

to leave his kingdom, he journeyed east and across the seas into exile. Ancient **prophecy** said he would return one day and reclaim his kingdom. Upon his return, the Aztec empire would fall.

During Montezuma's rule (1502–1520), the importance of this god was elevated. Montezuma was a lineal descendant on his mother's side of Quetzalcoatl. Quetzalcoatl had been a central deity for the ancient **Toltec** civilization. Montezuma at one time owned a painted book that chronicled a short history, mixed with mythology, confirming the belief that Toltec power was sanctioned by Quetzalcoatl. Therefore, the Toltec's ancient city of Tula (or Tollan) held great significance for Montezuma. Montezuma's reverence of the Toltec past led to a cultural shift during his tenure as emperor.

Montezuma's predecessors also held the ancient Toltecs in high esteem. In 1428, under the emperor Itzcoatl, the Aztecs descended on the ruins of nearby Tula and adopted the Toltec heritage as their own from what was left behind. Researchers believe the great city of Tula had been sacked and destroyed by an unknown people. Some Toltecs managed to escape and resettle elsewhere. Itzcoatl ordered any books that documented Toltec history to be burned. By erasing the Toltec history, the Aztecs were free to modify it and claim it as their own. Through these actions, the Aztecs "achieved what every successful people tries to do: they had established a grand history for themselves … the true heirs of the last great people of the valley, the Toltecs …"

With a homeland, origin story, and now history established, the Aztecs needed to create order and cohesion within their society. In order to do so, they developed two calendars. The first was an agricultural calendar, which covered 365 days. This agricultural calendar was called the ***xiuhpohualli***, and its days focused on the rituals related to seasonal agriculture. The second calendar was their sacred calendar, which covered 260 days. This calendar was called the ***tonalpohualli***, meaning "day count." It was used as a **divinatory** tool, focusing on the rituals related to their gods. These calendars were important in that they told the Aztecs when it was a good time to begin a harvest, start a journey, or declare war. After fifty-two years, the century ended, and a new one began.

Aztec life revolved around these calendars. They were integral for keeping track of the many ceremonies and festivals held throughout the year that correlated to specific gods. Several of these festivals involved human sacrifice and sometimes cannibalism. This required a supply of appropriate victims, which was often the catalyst for war with neighboring tribes. Many festivals were held to ensure there would be rain and ultimately abundant agriculture. For the growing capital city Tenochtitlán, and the expanding Aztec empire, this was important.

Though the Aztecs relied on their gods to protect them, they did not leave their agriculture to chance. They developed cultivation practices and diversified their food sources: **chinampa** agriculture, fruit and maize, game and fishing, and tribute from defeated enemies. Population growth and the need for food to sustain it put pressure on the land. Drought and famine were annual threats. The emperor would intervene as necessary to order sacrifices in hopes of thwarting threats to crops or opening the palace storehouses to the people during dire times.

Tenochtitlán was growing into a dominant and demanding city. Perched seven thousand feet up on the island within Lake Texcoco, there were limits to its growth—a reason to expand the empire. Tenochtitlán had been built over several generations, artificially extending the city over 2,500 acres (1,011 hectares) using stakes in the ground, filling in the gaps with mud and rocks. The Aztecs designed their capital city so that streets and canals led away from the temple precinct in all four directions. Drawbridges were used on the three **causeways** that connected Tenochtitlán to the mainland. These could be raised in defense if an enemy ever were to attack, cutting off invaders from reaching the capital. Tenochtitlán was considered impregnable—it had never been breached.

The safety of the capital city had been guaranteed due to a ninety-year alliance with two other cities, Tlacopan and Texcoco. These were more like satellite cities of Tenochtitlán. Together, they were known as the **Triple Alliance**. This alliance guaranteed a mutually advantageous **lacustrine** economy, which included not only the Triple Alliance but also about fifty small, self-governing city-states.

Tenochtitlán was symmetrically designed. The temple precinct was located in the center, within which the Great Temple for Huitzilopochtli stood. This temple was a 98-foot-high (30-meter-high) pyramid, with a rectangular base that was 382 feet (116 m) long and 262 feet (80 m) wide. On one side, one hundred fourteen steps rose almost vertically, ending at the top platform. The sanctuaries for **Tlaloc** (god of water/rain) and Huitzilopochtli stood on this platform. Sacrificial altars stood in front of each sanctuary. The temple of Quetzalcoatl stood 300 feet (91 m) to the east.

Merchants in the markets sold food items such as turkeys, rabbit, venison, beans, and vegetables. They also sold animal skins, cotton, salt, and wood. Knives made of **obsidian**, a dark, volcanic, glasslike rock, were available as was a variety of pottery. There were merchants who dealt with gold, silver, precious stones, feathers (which had religious significance), fabrics, and

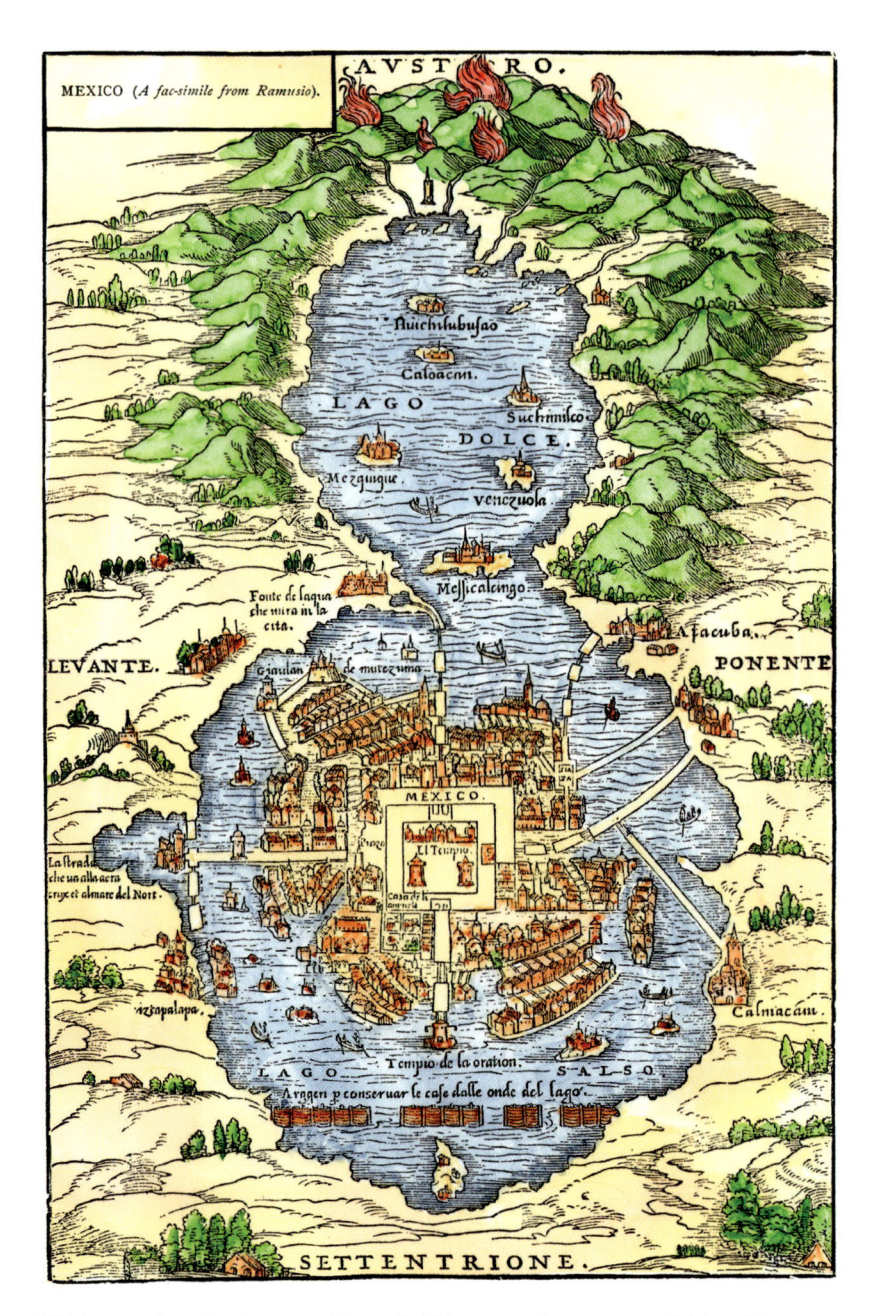

Within two hundred years, Tenochtitlán grew from a small island into an expansive city with a large population.

embroidery. Headdress makers, jewelers, stonecutters, and silver- and goldsmiths were considered high-status artisans.

With all of the canals, the citizens of Tenochtitlán used dugout canoes to travel throughout the city. Walking was the only other alternative. The only wheels the Aztecs used were for children's toys. They had not considered them for use in transportation.

Even though the Aztecs spent most of their time working, they also incorporated leisure activities into their lives. The many rituals, festivals, and celebrations were occasions during which people danced to music played with various pipes, rattles, whistles, flutes, and drums. Sporting events were for leisure but also sometimes revolved around worshipping their gods. A game similar to basketball called *ulama* was played. The stakes in this game were quite high. Only the nobility could play, and the losers were killed in sacrifice to the gods.

Aztec children did not have a lot of time to play games. Once old enough, they went to school. Though education was compulsory for everyone, girls went on to help their mothers keep the house and weave; boys were prepared for the military. All young men from ages eighteen to twenty-two served in the army. Boys either attended the **calmécac** or the **telpochcalli**. The calmécac was the "temple school" where the boys learned how to become priests or to take on high state offices. The telpochcalli was a "military school" where boys learned martial arts and war strategy, as well as public works and agriculture.

One might view the Aztecs as primitive; however, the Europeans who encountered them while discovering the New World were surprised at their advancements. The Aztecs had developed impressive systems for hygiene and sanitation—quite superior to some European cities during this same period.

They disposed of human waste in public privies or collected it from homes in dugout canoes. The Aztecs used steam baths to promote good health, and to ensure they had potable water in Tenochtitlán, they built **aqueducts** to bring water from springs on the mainland.

Over time, the Aztecs became more aristocratic, hierarchical, and imperialistic. The empire was ruled by the kings of the Triple Alliance. This alliance intimidated neighboring tribes, subjugating them to gain control. The Triple Alliance was always looking for a reason to declare war, especially if a town proclaimed their sovereignty and resisted their rule. The Aztecs allowed subjugated tribes to remain independent, governing and worshipping their own way as long as they accepted Huitzilopochtli as equal to their local deities. They could retain their gods, culture, and institutions, provided they met the Aztec demands of tribute. Tax collectors from Tenochtitlán came to collect on a regular schedule.

For some towns, tribute came in the form of food, materials, or gifts (feathers, precious stones, or gold). For others, tribute had to be paid in the form of prisoners. These prisoners were usually young warriors captured in battle for the sole purpose of serving as slaves and ultimately as sacrifices to the gods in Tenochtitlán. Conquered towns provided an endless supply of sacrificial victims.

Declaring war on a town to obtain sacrificial prisoners was a frequent tactic of the Aztecs. This type of war was called a War of Flowers (or **Garland War**). It was agreed upon in advance, and there was a specific process to be followed and rules that governed this type of warfare. A day was chosen, and on that day, the Aztec warriors would set off in procession to the town they decided to conquer. This procession consisted of priests, statues of the gods, and captains; soldiers followed the next day.

On the appointed day, warfare commenced in hand-to-hand combat. Aztec warriors had one goal only—to capture as many prisoners as possible for sacrifice. The first captives were sacrificed at the feet of the idols brought to the battlefield. This ensured Aztec victory. Once an Aztec warrior entered the enemy's temple precinct of their local god and set it on fire, the battle was over. The town was conquered.

Aztec Life Once Montezuma Came to Power

During Montezuma's reign, Tenochtitlán had become extremely powerful, imposing its will on much of Mexico. Many millions of people comprised the subjugated tribes who paid tribute to the capital city. Tribute helped the city prosper, but Tenochtitlán had also grown into a busy commercial center. Its sister city, Tlatelolco, located one mile (1.6 kilometers) north, was a semi-independent mercantile city that had become a great market. Everyone came to Tlatelolco's market to barter and trade goods.

Montezuma recognized the importance of the ***pochtecatl***, professional, long-distance traveling merchants who traded with people in faraway regions. By gaining access to new and distant territories, the pochtecatl were naturals for gathering intelligence on other tribes. With extensive knowledge of the far-reaching empire and outside lands, they were in an ideal position to spy on behalf of the Aztec emperor. This was important as Montezuma sought to maintain control of his vast empire.

Montezuma ushered in a cultural shift that strengthened the Aztec claims of Toltec lineage. As was customary for new emperors, Montezuma spent his first year in seclusion. During this time, he developed his Toltec plan. Desiring to return to the glories of the ancient Toltec civilization, Montezuma replicated

Ancient ruins from the Toltec civilization still stand in Tula, Mexico.

conditions he believed had been in place during their existence. Palace slaves who came into contact with him and his immediate family were replaced with nobles of Toltec descent. These removed slaves then served the nobles, performing menial tasks for them. Now that the burgeoning noble class had more responsibilities serving Montezuma, more slaves were needed.

Prior to this, slavery had not been an important part of Aztec society. In fact, slave-owning nobles were uncommon. But after 1502, when Montezuma became leader of the Aztecs, the nobles became busy in newly created positions close to power, and thus they required slaves to aid them in their daily lives. During this time, enslaving conquered enemies also was a new aspect of Aztec warfare. This was revolutionary within the palace.

These changes earned Montezuma the gratitude and support of the noble class. Within the first ten years of his reign, Montezuma had consolidated power, becoming the most autocratic and thus most powerful ruler in the history of the Aztec empire.

Challenges for Aztec Society

Montezuma had inherited a powerful empire. This did not come without challenges. Threats to agriculture were always a concern. As a trained priest, Montezuma read the Aztec books of fate and watched the skies for signs of omens and portents. Years of hardship due to drought and other strange events such as earthquakes, an unusual rat infestation, and even an eclipse overshadowed Montezuma's reign. Often, no matter how many ceremonies or sacrifices he ordered, Montezuma could not appease the gods. His belief that everything was preordained allowed him to accept events as the will of the gods.

Keeping the population of Tenochtitlán busy, cared for, and fed was a constant challenge. The Aztec system of tribute became more and more important. This in turn meant that tributes had to increase; demand required a steady supply. Tenochtitlán had grown dependent upon tribute. The city's population was focused on services and crafts. Supplies were needed and readily provided via tribute, which in turn made people view tribute as very necessary. Nobles had grown accustomed to certain delicacies obtained by tribute, such as tropical fruits and cocoa. Festivals and ceremonies grew more and more elaborate, needing gifts for the gods, decorations, and people to sacrifice. The citizens of Tenochtitlán had more and more needs that had to be maintained. More and more tribute was required to sustain these ever-growing needs.

With the increased demand for tribute placed on subjugated tribes, resentments grew across the empire. The Aztecs were almost always at war. They needed to assert their dominance across the empire as well as within their Triple Alliance, of which Montezuma was the undisputed head. At times, this was challenging, and they faced military setbacks, but overall, their faith in Huitzilopochtli and his promise of dominion over all of Mexico left the Aztecs undeterred. The Aztec empire expanded to ensure resources for their people, but, as most expanding empires experience, the habit of aggression is a hard one to break.

On top of the demands of a growing empire, nature always presented challenges that threatened their existence. In Aztec culture, the belief that any natural event was a sign from the gods—usually of displeasure—led them to increase sacrifices to avert disasters. In the end, they accepted whatever transpired as destiny. A sense of fate and predestination was ingrained in the Aztecs. Their lives were ruled by their books of fate.

In fact, the Aztecs were never sure if their world would survive at the end of each "century" (fifty-two-year cycle). They marked the occasion with a New Fire Ceremony, preceded by "tying up" the previous years. The prior fifty-two years were "bundled" into a cluster of fifty-two wooden rods, which symbolized each past year. The bundle was then ceremonially burnt to ashes. The ceremony began with twelve days of fasting on bread and water. The Aztecs went without making any fires. On the day when the star Aldebaran passed over the zenith at midnight, the Aztecs watched the sky and held their breath. If the star stood still, their world was about to end. If it continued moving, a sacrificial victim was killed, and the Fire Priest kindled a blaze over his heart. Torches were lit from this blaze and sent to all the temples in Mexico from which the people obtained fire for their domestic hearths. Life would continue for another fifty-two years.

The Aztecs, their gods, nature, and fate were all intertwined in a symbiotic relationship. As ruler, Montezuma routinely consulted the book of fate, the sacred texts, and the night skies for messages from the gods. Events took place in preordained cycles; he accepted the will of the gods without question.

Aztec expansion through military domination and religious imposition made them powerful. War and sacrifice were the normal process of life; however, those who were subjugated lived in fear. Over time, fear grew into resentment. Tribes resisted or rebelled. The Aztec empire was strong and crushed revolt. It seemed like nothing could stop the empire or topple Montezuma from power.

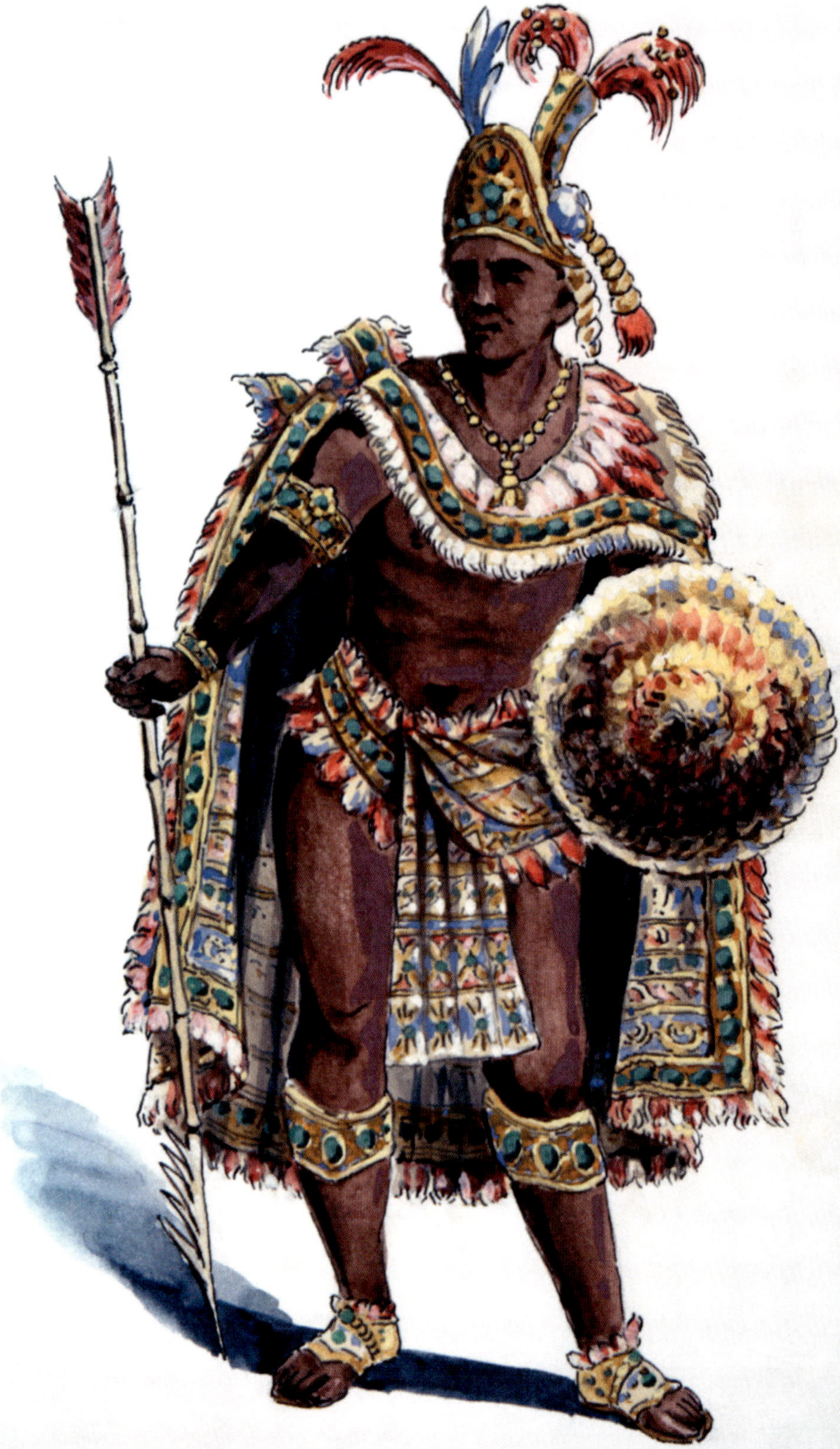

CHAPTER TWO
The Life of Montezuma

It can be difficult to study the lives of leaders from the ancient past because their lives were largely a mystery prior to the arrival of European explorers. Montezuma is no exception. Researchers and historians, however, can help us better understand these figures. For this book, much of Montezuma's early history comes from historians Cottie Arthur Burland and Hugh Thomas. Thomas's book *Conquest: Montezuma, Cortés, and the Fall of Old Mexico* depicts Montezuma as more of a three-dimensional individual:

> Montezuma was, like most Mexica, dark and of average height. His hair was wavy, his nose aquiline. He was well proportioned, spare, with a large head and somewhat flat nostrils. He seemed astute, wise and prudent; and in speech sharp, firm and eloquent … like most Mexica, he was courteous … That courtesy was necessary. Government depended on personal communication … Montezuma was a successful general before he came to the throne … he had also been for a time chief priest … Montezuma believed that the way to rule was to inspire people "with fear, not affection."

Opposite: Montezuma was destined from his birth to be a great leader of the Aztec empire.

Montezuma's Early Years Prepared Him for Leadership

Montezuma was, quite literally, born to be ruler of his people. Aztec priests consulted their books of magic after his birth in 1467. This particular year was dedicated to the god Quetzalcoatl. This dedication left an imprint on Montezuma, influencing his life's path. The Aztec belief in preordained fate meant that the year, day, and hour of one's birth determined individual destiny; no one could change the fate they were born into.

After his birth, the Aztec priests declared the baby Montezuma would be a future great ruler and high priest. Montezuma would possess infinite wisdom, which would guide him on his path to greatness. Eventually, this future ruler would die in glory for the gods. This life path was similar to the life of Quetzalcoatl while on Earth. This link to the god Quetzalcoatl defined Montezuma's life from the outset, setting him on a trajectory toward the most pivotal moment in Aztec history.

The Aztec calendar governed all aspects of life and was carved from solidified lava.

HISTORIAN OF MONTEZUMA, THE AZTECS, AND ANCIENT MEXICO

Cottie Arthur Burland, a British historian and author of *Montezuma: Lord of the Aztecs*, presents a more well-rounded perspective of the Aztec emperor compared to other sources. Burland purposely wrote about Montezuma from an Aztec point of view versus Spanish. Much of what is known about the Aztecs and Montezuma is presented through a Spanish filter. Burland gives a glimpse into Montezuma's life, who he was as a person, and subsequently, how he became a great leader.

Burland spent much of his forty-year career in the British Museum's Ethnography Department. Ethnography, an offshoot of anthropology, is the study of the customs of individual peoples and cultures. The author of more than forty books, Burland was a contributing writer for many others, as well as many publications, including the journal *Natural History*. Burland was also a fellow of the Royal Anthropological Institute. His writings covered topics such as ancient religions, primitive people and cultures, the ancient Americas, art, and mythology. His first work, *Gods of Mexico*, published in 1948, dealt with previously unexplored subject matter.

For his book about Montezuma, Burland referenced sources such as the **Codex** Aubin, Codex Xolotl, Friar Bernardino de Sahagun's *Historia General de las Cosas de la Nueva España*, and Spanish conquistador Bernal Diaz del Castillo's *The True History of the Conquest of New Spain*, among other works.

34 Montezuma II

When Montezuma was just two years old, his father, Axayacatl, became the ruler of the Aztec empire, taking over from the first Montezuma (Montezuma I). It was natural to assume that as the son of the Aztec emperor, Montezuma II would one day also become leader of the empire. But Aztec emperors did not follow a ruling line of father-to-son. The **Council of Four** had to elect the next emperor from among the families in the ruling class. However, the Aztec priests confirmed Montezuma would become a great ruler; all signs pointed to this future for the young prince.

Two-year old Montezuma spent the next year without his father. As was customary, Axayacatl went into seclusion for his first year in power. Emperor Axayacatl lived in a special building within the temple courtyard, fasting and meditating on the gods. This was the tradition, along with some ceremonial public appearances.

As a young child, Montezuma spent much of his time roaming the palace rooftop flower gardens, learning to sing and recite poems. Life was idyllic. As he grew older, Montezuma learned about the gods. He also heard stories about the warriors of Tenochtitlán. Instilling the importance of Aztec military might at a young age was the first step in preparing young Aztec boys for what lay in store for them as young men. Wars were always being waged, and Aztec boys were destined to fight. This was no different for the son of the emperor.

Montezuma was excited to go to school once he was old enough. He was especially happy to attend the calmécac, the temple school. Montezuma had a deep interest in learning about

Opposite: Here is a depiction of the god Quetzalcoatl (Feathered Serpent) with a headdress of Quetzal tail feathers and serpent tongue.

the gods, their worship, and how to interpret the signs of the universe (the signs of fate). He knew the calmécac would be a difficult experience. Students had to be brave when faced with the austerities demanded of them in order to achieve the lowest level of priesthood.

Students in the calmécac were expected to endure harsh conditions while they learned about and served the gods. They offered their suffering to the gods so that the gods would have mercy on the Aztec people. Enduring hardships served an additional purpose, hardening them for their futures as young warriors. While at the temple school, Montezuma experienced what every student experienced. He was treated no differently even though his father was the emperor.

Montezuma and his fellow students existed on a minimal diet: two tortillas and a cup of water each day. They slept on bare stone floors in the temple buildings. They were also expected to help the priests keep the temple clean. Montezuma performed his share of the daily chores just like the other students—there was no special treatment.

When he was ready, Montezuma participated in the first great test the students experienced: the night journey. Students could only participate in this test after progressing from cleaning the holy places. The night journey was part of the process for preparing the magic paints used by the priests to adorn their bodies. The paint was made up of calcified bodies of scorpions and other stinging insects, leaves from certain plants used for hallucinations, and greasy remains of burnt rubber. It was important to collect these ingredients at night, for it was

Opposite: Today, descendants of the Aztecs continue some of the traditions from the ancient past, such as dressing in ceremonial clothes and paints.

The Life of Montezuma 37

considered a magical time. A priest led each group of students out on the night journey because only the priests could recite the charms required to keep the powers of darkness away.

Montezuma learned about how important this magic body paint was for the priests. It deadened pain and allowed them to enter an elevated state of mind. Once in this elevated state, the priests performed sacred dances on the temple steps and human sacrifices to the gods. Once older and a priest, Montezuma would wear this same magic paint on his own body while taking part in sacred rituals.

As part of his priestly training, Montezuma needed to acquire the knowledge necessary to interpret the ancient calendars which predicted the fate of the Aztecs. He also needed to learn how to read the stars in the night sky. These skills enabled Aztec priests to understand the ways of the gods, foretell the future, and read the prophecies. Montezuma was especially attuned to the gods and the mysteries of the religion that formed their universe. He was skillful as an astronomer, and he watched for phenomena in the natural world that provided information from their gods.

Montezuma was a member of one of the three families from which the war leader of the Aztec nation would be selected. Naturally, he had to attend the telpochcalli, or military school. Aztec boys knew their history. Their patron god, Huitzilopochtli (god of the sun and war), had led their ancestors out of primitive poverty and into domination over all of Mexico in exchange for their faithfulness. Huitzilopochtli's importance to the Aztecs meant that war was an inevitable part of life. All young men from ages eighteen to twenty-two were required to become warriors.

Military school, in some small ways, was less rigorous than the temple school; boys slept on a grass mat with a thin cotton cloth as a cover. However, learning how to suffer was just as integral in military school as it was in the temple school. The purpose of suffering this time was to condition them to accept pain without uttering a sound. To the Aztecs, it was very important to meet one's death bravely and willingly. Showing fear of death was considered similar to treason and punishable by execution. Any warriors who were not courageous enough were purged from the ranks by such punishment.

In telpochcalli, groups of boys fought in mock combat, including Montezuma. This was an opportunity to earn a reputation as a ferocious warrior. Many boys suffered injuries, and some even died. They learned how to maneuver and handle war clubs (edged with obsidian blades) and how to use their shields. Students often earned serious cuts and scars during mock combat. Scars from battle were an important sign of brave warriors. These scars showed the world that the warrior had not run from battle to have their cuts immediately sewn up.

Students were also exposed to real battle. They followed the Aztec army on expeditions as porters. Carrying bundles of sandals, war clubs, and spears, the boys witnessed the rituals of battle firsthand. As a prince, Montezuma also had the opportunity to meet the older army commanders. It was important for him to learn strategy and the arts of commanding men. One day, he would be called upon to lead.

Montezuma was able to visit with his distant cousin, the ancient warrior Lord Tlacaelel. Tlacaelel had refused to become Aztec emperor three times because he wanted to continue leading forces to protect their great nation. Four Aztec emperors and army leaders called upon his knowledge. He advised on policy and military matters that had ensured the Aztecs continuous victory over many years. Montezuma gained much in knowledge from Tlacaelel about statecraft, military might, and the greatness of the empire.

At age sixteen, Montezuma and his fellow students were sent off to fight. They were expected to capture prisoners for sacrifice. Sacrifices were needed for the ceremonies that commemorated the first terrace of the new temple his father had been building for Huitzilopochtli. Targeting the hill town of Tzinancatepec, the students hid among rocks and brush in the evening while the **Ocelot** Warriors (one of the two special forces in the Aztec army) crept out ahead to spy and scout the land. In the morning, the war began.

The town's war chief and officials met the approaching Aztec army. War was not a sudden assault on an unsuspecting enemy; rules and rituals were the norm. The Aztecs demanded that the Tzinancatepecs pay tribute to the Aztec emperor in Tenochtitlán. They also expected their chief to be replaced by an Aztec governor and that on an annual basis, twenty men would be sent from the town for sacrifices to the gods.

The Tzinancatepecs did not receive these demands well. Their chief courteously expressed interest in friendship with the Aztec emperor but refused to offer his men for sacrifice. Both sides understood that war was the next course of action. This was Montezuma's first real battle.

The fighters of Tzinancatepec thought the fight would be easy. The central Aztec group was gathered tight and seemed small. However, they quickly discovered this assumption was wrong. Howls from the Aztec Ocelot Warriors emerged behind them as the Aztecs approached their rear flank. Historian Cottie Arthur Burland describes the fight that follows in his book, *Montezuma: Lord of the Aztecs*:

The Eagle and Ocelot Warriors were special armed forces who wore costumes depicting the animals they represented.

Warriors leapt at one another trying to batter down shields and weaken the enemy by cuts of the sharp obsidian club blades. If a man stumbled and fell he was likely to be seized, tied with a leather thong and dragged away. Montezuma saw some people fall, but suddenly he was parrying blows from a tall man much older than himself. He dodged and the two danced around each other. Then came a glancing cut which hurt, but the prince suddenly dived as his enemy towered over him for a final slashing blow. He swung his shield to deflect the blows and thrust the blunt end of his club under the ribs of the warrior. As the warrior doubled up in agony the boy swung his club, and just in time remembered to turn it to stun and not cut. Then slinging his shield to protect his neck in the melée he whipped a leather thong from his loincloth and tied the hands and feet of the unconscious warrior so that he could later be carried off for sacrifice.

Montezuma and other boys who had captured a prisoner in battle were now allowed to cut off the lock of hair that each had on the nape of their necks. This lock of hair was called the *piochtli*. It could not be cut until a boy had captured his first prisoner.

Before Montezuma graduated as a warrior, he returned to the temple school. This was the path for a future ruler. Montezuma was happy, since religion and astronomy were what he loved most, giving him a sense of purpose. He aspired to become the *Quetzalcoatl Totec Tlamacazqui* (one of the two high priests who reigned over Aztec religious life together). This high priest was in charge of the worship for Huitzilopochtli (the other was in charge of the worship for the rain god, Tlaloc). Becoming a high priest, however, did not mean Montezuma was excused from fighting when necessary.

Rising rapidly within the temple, Montezuma eventually became a sacrificing priest. In addition to his priestly duties, he was sometimes ordered out on military expeditions by his uncle Tizoc. Tizoc had been elected emperor after the death of Montezuma's father. These military expeditions were often to suppress local rebellions or keep the frontiers of the empire intact. Tizoc only ruled for three years before he died. Montezuma knew there was a possibility the Council of Four would name him as the next emperor. He felt a reluctance to leave his priestly duties and assume the responsibilities of leader; however, he was willing to do what was required and destined. As luck would have it, though, the Council chose another of his uncles, Ahuitzotl, to rule the empire. Montezuma resumed his focus on religion and astronomy.

As part of the ceremonies to honor the newly chosen Emperor Ahuitzotl, messages were sent to all the tribes in Mexico announcing the new leader and requesting gifts be sent in his honor. Many tribes and towns understood it was in their best interest to comply or else face reprisal from the Aztec armies. Eight tribes refused to send gifts. Once coronated, the newly installed Aztec emperor personally organized his armies to wage war against those eight tribes. He appointed Montezuma as one of his commanders to lead one hundred men.

Montezuma was well respected for his bravery. Known to be bold in battle, he led his men well. By now, Montezuma was wearing a special hairstyle reserved for seasoned warriors, his black hair bound in a crest on top of his head tied with a red leather thong. Only warriors who had taken four prisoners in battle were permitted to wear this hairstyle. The patterned cloak he wore signified that he had single-handedly taken prisoners; shoulder ornaments indicated the number taken. These outward symbols told the story of one side of Montezuma. He was a quiet and thoughtful man resulting from his training to be a priest. This made Montezuma seem somewhat mysterious. His interest in astronomy and the insight he could glean from the night skies often led him to wander outside alone at night to make observations. This was considered quite daring. But as a priest, Montezuma knew the charms to recite to ward off dangerous spirits that might threaten him.

During Ahuitzotl's reign, Montezuma experienced a lot of fighting. The emperor had a policy of vigorous conquest.

Montezuma, as an army commander, carried out this policy. It was important to Montezuma to be personally involved in expanding Aztec power and fulfilling his duty as a warrior by taking captives for Huitzilopochtli.

But life as a priest was also very important to Montezuma. When he was young and his father was emperor, he discovered a painted book among his father's possessions. This book detailed the history of the god Quetzalcoatl, the creation of the world, and Quetzalcoatl descending to Earth. It described the founding of Tula and the people, he believed, who were his ancestors (the Toltecs). Montezuma's training as a priest now allowed him to read and understand this book. He knew the prophecy of Quetzalcoatl's return. Montezuma's birth year had been dedicated to this god, and as a priest, he knew that his birth year would come around again in the Aztec calendar in 1518, a most significant year.

Determined to emulate the Toltec rulers, the Aztec ruling clan forged as many links as possible to the Toltec civilization—"their" ancient ancestors. When possible, marriages between remaining Toltecs with direct lineage to the old Toltec ruling class was most preferable. This would mean that each future prince would have more Toltec blood than those who came before. When it came time for Montezuma to marry, he hoped his wife would have Toltec ancestry. But this was not meant to be for his first wife. Though she descended from a ruling class, she was not of Toltec lineage. Nevertheless, he married and began his family. As was custom, Montezuma eventually married his second wife, who was a descendent of the Toltecs. These two women would remain his primary wives. Polygamy was acceptable for the nobles and leaders of the empire. Once Montezuma became emperor, he would have several concubines and many offspring.

Montezuma's Rise to Power

Despite endless wars, Montezuma's life became more settled. He was a family man, and he continued rising to higher military commands. Eventually, Montezuma became the Leader of Men (army commander in chief), and he was a popular commander. The year 1502 brought unexpected change, however. Emperor Ahuitzotl died suddenly from an accidental fall. The Council of Four deliberated, and it was decided that Montezuma should finally ascend to power and become the next Aztec emperor.

Montezuma accepted and became not only an elected ruler but also an autocrat, one with absolute power. He was the chairman of the Council of Four now—their Chief Authority. All of his training since he was a boy had led him to this position of rule. Montezuma had known that from his birth, he was predestined to this fate, for he was a descendant of the god-king Quetzalcoatl. Montezuma's duty now lay in protecting his people and his empire. He would ensure the protection of their ancient culture, encourage trade, and create a more unified empire under his command.

Now more than ever, Montezuma had to watch the skies for signs of the future as dictated to him by the gods. This was part of his job as emperor. Montezuma ascended to his palace rooftop at sunset, midnight, and sunrise to make his daily observations. Astrological work linked the messages from the skies to events unfolding on Earth. The Aztec people believed Montezuma to be a wise man. He had prophetic gifts, and the empire benefited from those gifts and his natural abilities as a leader.

As each ruler before him had, Montezuma spent his first year as emperor in seclusion. When he emerged, he had developed his Toltec plan and proceeded to implement it. He replaced his servants with nobles, recreating conditions believed to have been in place during ancient times when the Toltecs held power. Montezuma's other concern was obtaining prisoners for sacrifice to Huitzilopochtli and Tlaloc. He ordered his first war campaign specifically to capture sacrificial prisoners and slaves. Enslaving enemies was a new aspect in Aztec warfare under Montezuma. Now that he used nobles for his own servants, the nobles needed slaves to assist them with menial tasks.

The Aztec empire was at the height of its power. Montezuma was always in consultations, meeting with the Council as well as Tenochtitlán community leaders. People filled the palace waiting for an audience with the emperor. When it was their turn, they would speak quietly to Montezuma, never looking him in the eyes. Montezuma would respond in a low voice. Courtesy was maintained. Wherever he went within the city, he was greeted with extravagant respect.

Challenges Facing Montezuma as Emperor

Maintaining the vast Aztec empire was a regular challenge for Montezuma, one that he had the most power to control because of his powerful armies. However, other challenges, such as environmental issues, proved more difficult and tested him as emperor. Crops were often threatened; the book of fate warned that the year 1504 would bring drought. To avert this disaster, Montezuma dedicated a new temple to Cinteotl, the spirit of the maize crop. Sacrifices were made. Yet all signs continued to point to impending drought. The gods did not respond positively to Montezuma's acts of reverence. In fact, 1504 was a year of misfortune. Montezuma searched the skies for answers, but none were to be had. Shooting stars from the east gave Montezuma a feeling of foreboding.

Effects from the drought were really felt in 1505, when the fields produced no food. As emperor, Montezuma opened the army and palace storehouses to aid his people. He sent messengers to a neighboring tribe requesting food, though it was not enough for Tenochtitlán's large population. No matter what Montezuma did to appease the gods, they did not listen. No doubt he found this troubling, but Montezuma accepted the will of the gods; glory or disaster of the empire was at their mercy. Another ruler might have ordered actions to aid in crop production such as extending the aqueducts to bring in fresh water, but Montezuma was a strong believer in preordained fate. If it was the gods' will to suffer drought, then so be it.

The year 1506 finally brought rain, which improved crop production for the Aztecs. This year was also significant for Montezuma. He presided over the end of a fifty-two-year era. The Aztecs, including Montezuma and the Council of Four, suffered during the obligatory twelve-day fast. The priests and Montezuma watched the sky and the passage of stars. They made their observations and deliberated as to whether or not the world was coming to an end or if the sun would rise again. Once it was known that the world would not end, the New Fire Ceremony began to mark the new fifty-two-year era, or "new bundle of years."

This new era started with good news for Montezuma. The alliance between two neighboring tribes, the Tlaxcalans and Uexotzino, was finished. The Tlaxcalans were particularly rebellious. They had taken every opportunity to fight the Aztecs, refusing subjugation. The Aztecs viewed the Tlaxcalans as a steady supply of sacrificial prisoners, which the Tlaxcalans deeply resented. Seizing a prime moment, Montezuma plotted an attack on them.

Montezuma's attack on Tlaxcala was well organized and successful, leading to a treaty. Tlaxcalans's lands remained intact, but many prisoners were taken for sacrifice. After this victory, Montezuma negotiated peace with the Uexotzino. He could be ruthless when expanding Aztec dominion over various tribes and territories. He even went so far as to exterminate a tribe that rebelled against his tax collectors, who were collecting annual tribute. If a tribe plundered another tribe's tribute meant for Tenochtitlán, Montezuma responded with military force.

By 1512, Montezuma had grown uncommunicative and disturbed. Visions of a coming disaster plagued him. Over the prior six years, omens had come to him in the form of an eclipse, a comet, and three earthquakes. Montezuma was convinced that the god Quetzalcoatl was returning. Quetzalcoatl's return date was anticipated once in every era; this date was scheduled to come around again in 1518. Montezuma became conflicted. He knew the Quetzalcoatl prophecy; no amount of sacrifices or wars could change fate. Montezuma's preordained end would come with Quetzalcoatl's return.

Despite his gloominess, Montezuma was at the height of his glory as emperor. The Aztecs ruled the land. People obeyed them even if they did not necessarily like them. But there were always some exceptions.

By late 1518, "wooden houses with white wings" were spotted along the eastern Mexican coast. Montezuma's visions continued. In early 1519, messengers reported back to him of strangers from the sea. Stories of these strangers coming ashore and fighting with gray swords that proved to be deadly unsettled Montezuma. He was told about the strange **tepuztli** (Nahuatl word for copper) that released "thunder and lightning" and smashed trees apart (guns). The strangers rode the backs of "deer without horns" and charged people with spears (riders on horseback).

Montezuma was well aware that sometimes the gods assumed the form of men, and that Quetzalcoatl had once been a man himself in ancient Tula, and this troubled him. Everything these strangers from the sea did was reported back to Montezuma. Their presence affected his ability to rule. He fell into depression, unsure what to do. The fate of the great Aztec empire rested in his hands, and his future decisions would be pivotal.

Montezuma faced a dilemma. He knew what fate had in store, but he was not willing to voluntarily hand power back to Quetzalcoatl. He decided the only thing he could do was delay the god's victory.

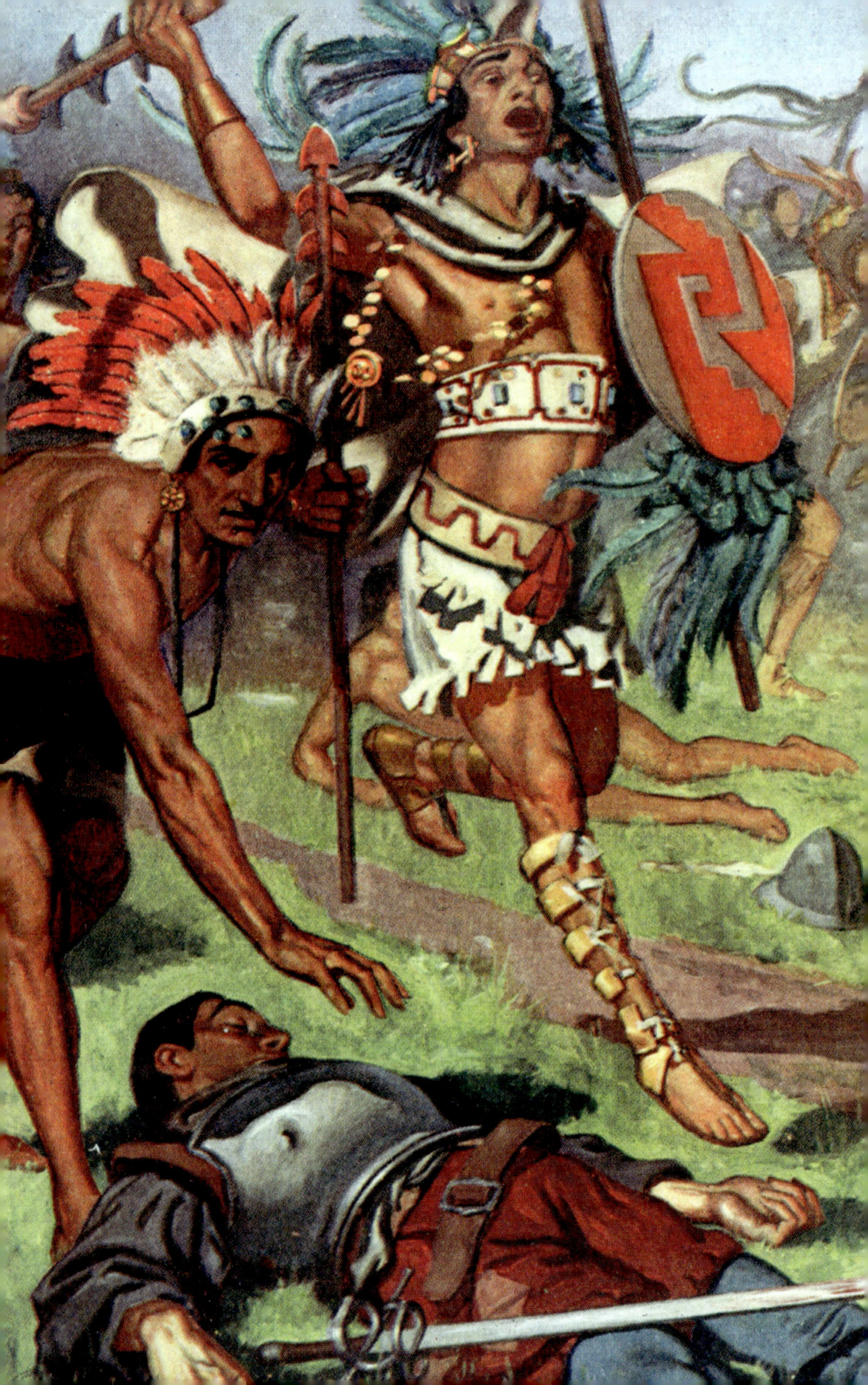

CHAPTER THREE

Waging War

Montezuma's most well-known conflict was with the Spanish conquistadors between 1519 and 1520 CE. This clash of empires was not necessarily a war, nor was it a specific battle. Rather, it was a chain of events that unfolded over a year's time. Some research implies that the outcome was a failure on the part of Montezuma. Or was it? Montezuma understood the portents as well as his own destiny. Did he maneuver things to meet an end beyond his control and spark a desired outcome for his people? Or did his unwavering belief in the gods and fate make him blind to see alternative options? This, Montezuma's most famous conflict, has been presented by historians from different perspectives.

The Conflict

Montezuma's messengers had kept him informed and updated about the "ugly creatures" that came from the sea. He did not know they were Spanish, but he did know the prophecy of the god Queztzalcoatl and his impending return. He also knew that if this happened while he was emperor, his time as ruler over the

Opposite: Aztec warriors engage in battle with Spanish conquistadors led by Hernán Cortés.

This painting shows Hernán Cortés and his conquistadors arriving on the eastern coast of Mexico at Vera Cruz.

Waging War

empire would be over. Montezuma received reports on everything these strangers did. Burland, in his book *Montezuma: Lord of the Aztecs*, describes impressions the Spanish left upon Montezuma's messengers, which were conveyed back to him:

> The strange beings were not gentle. Their ferocity knew no bounds: they killed the people before them and made no attempt to take prisoners for sacrifice. They made horse shouting and not whistling as they attacked. They seemed almost invincible, and it was clear that magic must be used if they were to be brought within the control of Mexico.

Montezuma was not yet sure what the intentions were of these men. He needed more information before deciding to wage any kind of battle. This was different than sending armies out to conquer neighboring tribes. Normal warfare practices would not apply to this unusual situation.

Montezuma's Military Leadership Style

To Montezuma, war followed strict traditions. The Aztecs cared about formality when challenging and beginning war. Sometimes, the emperors led armies into battle. Often the war leader was a great nobleman. He served as the Keeper of the Arsenal. Under this leader, there would be a group of commanders, youth leaders, and masses of conscripted warriors. Sometimes armies from several tribes joined the Aztecs in battle. These tribes were led by experienced generals who were known to work well together.

Lastly, the Aztec army had two special forces of warriors, the Ocelot Warriors and the Eagle Warriors. A man had to be specially chosen to join the ranks of these two warrior groups.

Two vastly different civilizations collided when the Aztecs and the Spanish finally met.

Selection depended upon a warrior's dedication to the service of the sun (Huitzilopochtli) and sponsorship by members with proven valor. These two forces served different purposes in battle. The Ocelot Warriors were scouts who fought the flanks of the enemy, while the Eagle Warriors usually consisted of nobles who attacked down the center of the enemy's army. Ordinary warriors

Waging War 55

AZTEC MILITARY TECHNOLOGY

The technology used by the Aztecs in warfare was suitable for how they waged war against other Mexican tribes. For the Aztecs, the purpose of waging war was to subjugate tribes and capture as many prisoners as possible for future sacrifice. Killing opponents on the battlefield was not part of their strategy. Therefore, the Aztec weaponry and war tactics were designed around this purpose. War clubs were used to stun opponents. Clubs with sharp obsidian blades were wielded to wound, not kill. To protect themselves against cuts, the Aztecs did not wear chain mail or armor; instead, they soaked their clothing in a salt solution that made the fabric stiff to thwart a blade. They also padded their clothing with cotton, which was effective against arrow attacks. In the Mexican climate, cotton clothing was cooler than armor.

In addition to the war clubs and obsidian blades, Aztec weapons included the javelin, arrows, slings, stones, spears, and hatchets. However, this technology was no match for the Spanish's steel swords and armor, soldiers on horseback, skilled **harquebusiers** (firearm-wielding soldiers), and cannons. Additionally, facing an enemy who did not fight like Mexican tribes hindered Aztec effectiveness. Their wartime strategy, to maim and capture versus killing opponents, affected the way they used their technology, eventually costing them in the heat of battle against the Spanish.

Opposite: The *atlatl* provided leverage to fling light spears farther and faster than by hand-throwing.

Waging War 57

Costumed Ocelot and Eagle Warriors wielded obsidian-edged clubs and shields in warfare.

engaged in general fighting in which one army was pushed back until heavy losses led that army's leaders to seek a parley, a discussion or conference, on the terms for surrender.

From the Ocelots and Eagles came an elite special force made up of volunteers. These volunteers had one thing in common: they were chosen from the Masters of Cuts. This distinction was awarded to those warriors who had, in one battle, taken three enemies alive for sacrifice. These elite warriors were prepared to take captives or die trying, and die many of them did. They did not carry war clubs or shields but rather rushed into battle naked except for an open cloak made of strong rope netting. This was what they used to capture and carry their enemies off—alive.

Montezuma's vast experience as a young warrior and eventual army commander was invaluable to him. He became intimately acquainted with the geography of the empire during his service in the Aztec army. Montezuma drew upon this firsthand knowledge of battle when wielding his power as emperor to conquer tribes and territories, and to assert Aztec power. It would be fair to say that Montezuma and the Aztecs had little experience in losing when it came to battle.

Still, even with his experience and the military might of his armies, Montezuma was cautious with these new arrivals, these strangers from the sea. These men representing Spain were conquistadors, or conquerors. Seeking out new territories in the New World, these particular Spaniards arrived on the eastern coast of Mexico from across the seas. Montezuma received reports about the newcomers on a regular basis. They seemed to be settling on shore. Unsure if this was the returning god Quetzalcoatl, Montezuma did not want to attack. He alerted the tribes along and near the coast to treat the strangers as if they were *tecuhtli* (great lords). Montezuma hoped that the strangers would be persuaded to stay on the coast and not advance inland.

Waging War 59

He hoped to achieve this by having the local tribes treat the visitors well and give them gifts. If this really was Quetzalcoatl returning, Montezuma's plan was to delay the incoming deity from reaching Tenochtitlán.

Montezuma learned more about the leader of these strangers from the various intelligence reports that he received from the coast. He was "a man of strange pale colour with black beard and hair. He had landed in black tights and gloves, like the black paint worn by priests, and by Quetzalcoatl himself. He wore a body covering with a chain of gold from which was suspended a white shell cameo: the wind-jewel of Quetzalcoatl; and on his head was the flat-topped Huaxtec hat of a type always worn by Quetzalcoatl. It was obvious that the god had arrived."

Montezuma decided he had to act. He sent emissaries with gifts to meet the strangers on the coast. Hernán Cortés, the leader of the Spaniards, received Montezuma's emissaries and treated them with courtesy. He invited them onto his ship and accepted their gifts of food, jewels, and gold but wanted to know why they gave him so little of it (the Spanish were greedy for gold). Cortés also wanted to know when he could meet the emperor Montezuma so he could introduce him to the one true faith of Christianity.

When communicating with tribes encountered on his travels, Cortés used two translators, a man and a woman. The woman was young, dressed in Aztec fashion, and knew the languages of the Aztec empire. This knowledge enabled her to communicate with the Aztecs first in Nahuatl and then in Mayan with her co-translator, Gerónimo de Aguilar. He would then translate in Spanish for Cortés.

This woman was born Ce Malinalli (La Malinche), but Cortés and his men called her Doña Marina. Over time, Doña Marina would become very important to Cortés; her translations and her influence played a role in the events that eventually transpired. Over time, she learned Spanish, which made Gerónimo de Aguilar obsolete. Cortés began to use only Doña Marina for important communications between himself and the Aztecs. Montezuma must have been aware that her given name, Ce Malinalli, meant the "bringer of misfortune." Always on the lookout for portents and omens, her presence must have added to Montezuma's sense of unease about these strangers.

Though initially courteous, Cortés had Montezuma's emissaries tied up. The Spanish conquistadors demonstrated their power using the cannons that they had brought with them. No one in Mexico, including the Aztecs, had seen such weaponry. When the Spanish fired the cannons, it terrified Montezuma's emissaries.

Eventually, the emissaries escaped in the night and returned to Tenochtitlán with a lot to report to Montezuma. They described the gods and talked of Quetzalcoatl. They had seen gray stone that was metal, harder than bronze. They told Montezuma about the strange deer without horns and the fierce dogs. They described how the strangers could harness the power of lightning and use it as a weapon. Montezuma pondered these reports. Quetzalcoatl was changed and now a threat to Huitzilopochtli. He also knew that the returned god would be victorious while he, himself, would face defeat.

When Cortés came ashore in April 1519, the Totonac tribe that inhabited the eastern coast greeted him warmly. They were already familiar with the Spanish from prior expeditions. They also educated Cortés about the Aztecs and how they operated, conquering tribes and exacting tribute. Cortés was pleased to learn that the subjugated tribes resented the Aztecs deeply.

Hernán Cortés journeyed inland from the eastern coast of Mexico to personally meet Montezuma.

Montezuma Employs Strategy against the Spanish

Armed with the knowledge of gold and tribal resentments against the Aztecs, Cortés decided to go meet Montezuma. He embarked on a journey inland through the Aztec empire.

With spies everywhere, Montezuma received word that Cortés was on the move. He routinely sent messengers to meet with the Spanish leader to persuade him that traveling to Tenochtitlán would be an impossible and arduous journey. He also employed Aztec magicians to use all of their power to impede and frighten off the Spanish. However, magic did not work.

Setting off in August 1519, Cortés encountered difficulties along the journey to Tenochtitlán. Not all tribes were as welcoming as the Totonacs, who were their first allies. The Spanish arrived in the territory of the Tlaxcalans. Used to defending themselves against the Aztecs, the Tlaxcalans were not going to let these strangers crush them either. There was much fighting between the fierce tribe and the Spanish, but each side gained respect for each other's strength. The Tlaxcalans saw an opportunity for revenge against the Aztecs by joining forces with the Spanish. Fighting ceased, and an alliance was formed. Some of the Tlaxcalan nobles even became baptized Christians. These new allies gave Cortés insight into just how despised the Aztecs were amongst many of the subjugated tribes.

Montezuma continued to send messengers in an attempt to dissuade the Spanish from coming to Tenochtitlán. Cortés insisted he wanted to meet Montezuma in person. Montezuma was conflicted, and therefore sent mixed messages. He expressed hospitality to these strange gods, but he also urged them to turn back. Montezuma was concerned because the strangers had not been affected by the magicians and their powers. He could only conclude that their divine protection was because it was indeed Quetzalcoatl, returning after five hundred years in exile.

It took Cortés and his men two months to finally reach Tenochtitlán. The Aztecs did not quite know what to make of the Spanish. The Spanish wore gray suits (armor) and looked strange. The despised Tlaxcalans were with them. Montezuma and Cortés met on the causeway that led into Tenochtitlán. Montezuma bowed a little and welcomed Cortes in his quiet voice.

Cortés greeted Montezuma and made overtures of friendship. Both leaders exchanged gifts before Montezuma and his entourage headed back into Tenochtitlán. Cortés and his entourage walked with them side-by-side. Montezuma provided accommodations to Cortés and his men in the palace of Axayacatl, his father's old palace.

During their first night in Tenochtitlán, the Spanish kept constant watch. They had seen the crowd of Aztecs watch them enter their city. They noticed the animosity between the Aztecs and the Tlaxcalans. They wondered if they had walked into a trap. The next day, Montezuma showed Cortés his own palace. They also engaged in talks. Cortés attempted to explain his role as an emissary from a great king across the seas (King Charles V of Spain). Cortés explained that he had been sent to bring knowledge of the "true" religion to the Aztec people. Montezuma was confused as to why a god would refer to himself as just an emissary.

Montezuma was willing to pay tribute to this king across the seas if someone came to collect it. He felt this might persuade Cortés to leave the empire, knowing they would receive an annual tribute. Montezuma knew of their greed for gold, which the Aztecs thought was strange—they thought gold was beautiful, but they did not value it in the same way. In Aztec culture, feathers were considered far more valuable than gold. Montezuma believed if he could offer enough gold, Cortés and his men would leave. What Montezuma failed to understand was that gifts of gold only increased their desire to stay.

On another day, Montezuma took Cortés to see the Great Temple. Montezuma did not know that Cortés wanted to replace their idol of Huitzilopochtli with the Christian cross. Cortés threatened to destroy the Huitzilopochtli idol if the Aztecs continued to perform human sacrifices to honor it. This shocked Montezuma. It was blasphemy for the returned god Quetzalcoatl to demand that his rival, Huitzilopochtli, be destroyed.

Montezuma grew anxious and conflicted about Cortés. Cortés worried that he and his men were outnumbered. He grew more concerned once news of an Aztec attack on the Totonacs at the coast resulted in the deaths of some of the men he had left behind. Cortés worried they would now be easily killed or worse, taken for human sacrifice at the top of the Great Temple.

Montezuma Makes a Mistake, or Does He?

The uprising at the Spanish settlement on the coast at **Vera Cruz** prompted Cortés to ensure that he and his men would not be harmed. Feeling desperate, Cortés decided he needed to take a prisoner. This prisoner would be Montezuma. Cortés wrongly believed that the Aztecs would respond to a captive Montezuma in the same manner European peasants would if their king was kidnapped. He had no knowledge of how the Aztecs chose their

In an act of appeasement, Montezuma willingly submitted to be under the control of Cortés.

66 Montezuma II

emperors, and he assumed it was as he knew it to be in Spain. But Cortés could not just take Montezuma prisoner. He had to lure the emperor under false pretenses and then keep him captive.

Cortés asked to speak with Montezuma. He was granted this request. The Spaniard, along with his fully armed men, marched to meet with the emperor. Cortés was very courteous and invited Montezuma to be his guest at the old palace of Axayacatl. Montezuma did not respond to this offer. His silence angered the Spaniards, who accused him of planning the attack on the Spanish settlement at Vera Cruz. Montezuma knew at this moment that he was caught in a trap. It was important for him to delay his preordained fate. He knew he was being taken captive and there was no hope for him to survive what was to come next. He also knew if there was an insurrection, the Spanish would kill him. Montezuma wasn't ready to die just yet.

Montezuma was now hostage in his own capital city. To control the situation, he conveyed to his people that he was spending time with the Spanish in their accommodations at his own choosing. Yet, the Aztecs knew something was not right with this situation. Montezuma was kept under guard in his father's palace yet he was permitted to continue to perform his duties as emperor. The Spanish treated him with courtesy, and Montezuma was kind to his captors.

This extraordinary situation continued for half a year. The Spanish were a small minority within Tenochtitlán and could easily be cut off from the mainland. They held in their power the great leader of the Aztec empire. He was their hostage but treated well. Montezuma remained calm throughout his situation. He continued his duties, giving orders, and directing policy that was in the best interests of the empire and their gods. This was a most challenging time for Montezuma. He did not want to be

Waging War **67**

dethroned, but he also did not want to go against the gods' wishes and his own fate.

Even though Montezuma could continue his duties as emperor, he faced limitations. He still needed to preside over ceremonies, and for that, Montezuma had to persuade Cortés to allow him to do so. After all, this was his role as a high priest and emperor. Cortés accompanied Montezuma as he took part in a sacrifice and was horrified. Cortés ordered that all human sacrifice must come to an end. Montezuma warned that there would be a full Aztec revolt if anything interfered with their worship of their gods, including the sacrifices that kept their world going. Montezuma offered a concession, allowing the Spanish to take over the Temple of Tlaloc as their holy space. Cortés erected the Christian cross and created a new chapel. The Spanish now had a foothold. The Aztecs worried that the desecration of Tlaloc's temple would lead to devastating drought and starvation.

Montezuma never stopped urging Cortés to accept tribute and leave Mexico. Cortés falsely assured Montezuma that he would leave when ships came for him. The Spanish stayed in Tenochtitlán for seven months before a chain of events would lead to Montezuma's most famous conflict and a clash of civilizations.

One day, Montezuma received a messenger who gave him a sheet of painted cotton. It showed images of ships arriving at the coast. Montezuma knew the day had come for the Spanish to leave Tenochtitlán. He showed this message to Cortés, reinforcing that now they could leave Mexico with a tribute for their king across the seas. Montezuma was surprised that Cortés did not look happy. In fact, he looked disturbed.

Cortés had embarked on his journey to Mexico from Cuba illegally. He feared the governor of Cuba, Diego Velásquez, would send ships after him to arrest him and take control of Mexico from him. It now appeared an invasion force had indeed come for him. Cortés felt threatened; his accomplishments in Mexico were at risk. He needed to take action and repel the invaders.

Cortés divided his men, taking some with him for a return to his coastal settlement in Vera Cruz. He left about one-third of his men behind in Tenochtitlán to guard Montezuma and maintain their foothold within the capital city. Cortés chose to leave his lieutenant, Pedro de Alvarado, in command of the men left behind, a fateful decision. Alvarado was strong and brave but extremely volatile.

With Cortés away, the Tlaxcalans whispered in Alvarado's ear about the Aztecs. They told him of plots afoot to ambush the diminished Spanish contingent. Alvarado took their warnings to heart, seeing the Aztecs in Tenochtitlán from a different perspective. He now saw signs of possible danger everywhere for himself and his men.

Montezuma continued carrying out his duties as emperor while still under Spanish guard. The Aztecs were preparing for the upcoming important spring festival of Toxcatl to celebrate Huitzilopochtli. Montezuma sought permission from Alvarado to continue with this festival and received his consent. However, Alvarado became disturbed once the festival began. Aztec war leaders and warriors filled the square for dances to honor their god. This large gathering of Aztec warriors spooked Alvarado. He had not understood the purpose of the festival. This gathering of the Aztec military, coupled with the warnings from the Tlaxcalans, made Alvarado perceive the event as a threat. He also saw an opportunity to destroy the leadership of the Aztec forces and as many warriors as possible.

An Uneasy Peace Is Broken

Alvarado issued orders to his men. The harquebusiers positioned themselves at the tops of the palace walls. The rest of the Spanish surrounded the square.

Alvarado gave the order, and his men charged the Aztec warriors on horseback, steel blades at the ready. The Aztecs were not expecting this. The gathering in the square turned into a massacre.

When Montezuma learned of this massacre, he did not respond. He fell into a deep gloom. Fate was preordained, and he knew he must accept it. But the Aztecs who survived the massacre had had enough. They had grown tired of remaining passive toward the Spanish. Montezuma realized he was no longer an effective leader. His people were most likely aware by now that their emperor was under Spanish control.

Montezuma's religious training informed him that when his fifty-two years were completed, the cycle of his personal fate would also be completed—ending, most likely, with his death. Montezuma requested permission to meet with his brother Cuitláhuac (who had also been under Spanish guard along with other nobles). What the brothers discussed is not known. Montezuma made sure their meeting was secret and took place in front of guards who did not understand their language. The events that followed suggest Montezuma had been preparing for his own death. It is possible he gave his approval for the Council of Four to depose him and replace him with a new emperor.

Montezuma realized he had been rendered completely powerless. The peace he had tried to maintain, placating himself to the Spanish, had resulted in the massacre of his people. Montezuma played the last card he had as a great military leader. He took himself officially out of power. This would allow a new leader to rise and rebel against the Spanish invaders. The Council of Four met to discuss Montezuma and what he had asked of his brother Cuitláhuac. Cortés, and the Spanish, failed to understand how the Aztecs' emperors came to power. They assumed sovereign rule was passed from father to son. It was with that assumption that Cortés felt holding Montezuma hostage would allow him to control the Aztec population.

While still on the coast, Cortés received reports about the massacre in Tenochtitlán. Alvarado had written to inform him that the Aztecs had attacked them; they had no choice but to respond. Cortés, having defeated the invading force from Cuba, made the return trip to Tenochtitlán. He arrived back in the capital city on June 24, 1520.

Upon their arrival, the Spaniards were met with silence. The Aztecs remained hidden and kept to themselves. Even the great market, Tlatelolco, was closed. Needing resources, Cortés demanded that Montezuma open the market. Montezuma responded that he could do nothing but that his brother Cuitláhuac, if released, could assist. Cortés agreed to this arrangement, unaware that Cuitláhuac had been against allowing the Spanish into Tenochtitlán in the first place. Once free, Cuitláhuac began to organize the Aztec resistance.

The very same day, random attacks were carried out against the Spanish throughout the city. Cortés received word that the Aztecs were preparing for war. The Spanish were surrounded. They were ambushed wherever the Aztecs found them, shooting arrows and throwing stones. They set fire to the old palace of Axayácatl, but Spanish harquebusiers kept them at bay from the inside.

There were several days of skirmishes. At dawn, the Spanish ventured out to try to secure nearby houses and expand their perimeter, but the Aztecs would push them back and retake the houses. Inside the palace, the Spanish were running out of drinking water. It was dangerous to walk through the palace courtyard as Aztecs hurled stones into the space: "Possession of cannon no longer made much difference … Superior technology did not count in street battles … all [Mexica/Aztecs] just fought as best they could, without many orders, but with instinctive discipline, with general guidance from Cuitláhuac and the few other leaders who had survived Alvarado's massacre."

Though most Aztecs fought to kill, which was an unusual tactic for them, some captured Spanish soldiers were dragged up the temple steps for immediate sacrifice to the sun. This horrified and terrified the Spanish. Cortés tried to persuade Montezuma that it was in the best interest of the Aztecs to cease their attacks on the Spanish. Montezuma knew Cortés was only concerned for himself and his own men. Even though he knew he no longer held power over his own people, Montezuma finally acquiesced to Cortés's request. He ascended to the parapet of the palace wall to stand before the Aztecs.

Montezuma Makes the Ultimate Sacrifice for His Nation

When the Aztecs saw Montezuma, a hush fell over them. After a minute or two of silence, voices called out "coward!" and "traitor!" Montezuma spoke loudly, telling his people that the Council of Four had elected Cuitláhuac in his place. He no longer held authority over them. All was silent until "a swishing sound as one, two, three stones came flying through the air. One struck the crown from his head, one struck his cheek and another his forehead. Without a word he fell to the ground."

The Aztecs dispersed. The stoning of Montezuma by his own people must have stunned Cortés and the Spaniards who witnessed it. They realized their valuable hostage was no longer security for their own safety. Montezuma, alive but gravely injured, was hurried back to his quarters in the old palace. He refused to lie down or accept bandages for his wounds. Knowing the Aztecs did not fight at night, Cortés took the opportunity to burn as many houses as he could to prevent the warriors from using the rooftops to throw stones at his men. Fighting continued.

Three days after being stoned, Montezuma died of his wounds, having suffered stoically. It is important to note that there are different accounts of what happened next: the Spanish version and the Aztec version. The Spanish claim they spoke with the new emperor, Cuitláhuac, and returned Montezuma's body to him with honor. The Aztecs claim that in the middle of the night, a palace doorway opened and the bodies of Montezuma and his nephew were dumped outside. Montezuma's body showed signs that he had been stabbed.

The Aztecs continued fighting against the Spanish. Cortés knew they needed to escape the city. Their food was limited, their gunpowder was low, and the palace that was their only protection was riddled with holes. He had requested parleys with Cuithláhuac, offering to return looted Aztec treasure if allowed to leave Tenochtitlán with his men. These requests fell on deaf ears. On June 30, 1520, Cortés made the decision to retreat from the city at midnight. The Spanish made a portable wooden bridge to aid in crossing gaps in the causeway that could trap them.

Their escape went well until they made it to the outskirts of the city. A woman retrieving water spotted them. She sounded

Waging War

the alarm. The Aztecs were roused from sleep and took to their canoes. They paddled swiftly to intercept the Spanish fugitives:

> Suddenly there was a splashing of thousands of paddles as canoes stormed across the lake. The bridges were pulled down, and the Spaniards were attacked from all sides . . . Warriors leaping from canoes tried to drag their enemies into the lake and drown them. Others harassed the rear, killing the wounded as they fell back . . . As the Spanish party advanced to the gaps in the causeway, they fought each step. Some fell into the waters, some scrambled or leapt fighting across the gap . . . Many were cut down, others dropped their loads in the marshy lake bed . . . the piles of dead increased; the Aztecs were not pausing to select prisoners for sacrifice.

The Spanish who attempted to flee Tenochtitlán with gold most likely died. The weight of the precious metal slowed them and led to drowning if they fell into the canals or a lake. Much treasure was lost during the Spanish retreat and in the melée that occurred. By the time the surviving Spanish reached safety, Cortés realized two-thirds of his men were either missing or dead. He referred to this night as *la noche triste*, or the "night of sorrows."

The Aztecs were not finished with their attack. Their plan was to continue to harass the Spanish as they retreated until they arrived at a suitable location to massacre them. The Spanish retreated toward the hills. They needed to return to Tlaxcala and regroup. Before they could get to what they hoped would be safety, a great Aztec army with war banners and featherwork appeared. They had come to destroy the Spanish once and for all. However, Cortés had spent enough time with the Aztecs, observing them and their behaviors, that he knew the habits of the Aztec army. The formality and fighting style of the Aztecs, though dominant against neighboring tribes, had been untested against outside enemies (from across the sea). Cortés knew the army always paused before any attack. This gave him the opportunity to see where the Aztec army commander was—in the center, directing the movements of the Ocelot and Eagle Warriors:

> Cortés called his horsemen to form up and to strike a path through the enemy and to kill or at least upset the commander. When the attack began, all the Spanish horsemen were wounded, but nevertheless the assault got through. The golden palanquin was upset, the commander trampled and wounded, and his golden standard was carried off by a Spanish horseman back to Cortés. Demoralization set in among the Aztecs, some warriors stood and fought, others scattered.

Upon arriving at Tlaxcala, the Spanish were met by the chiefs. They had learned of the battle of Otumba with the Aztecs and the destruction of Montezuma, their enemy. They welcomed the Spanish. Cortés would use his time in Tlaxcala to recover from the defeat of battle, replenish his military stores, and prepare his return to take Tenochtitlán.

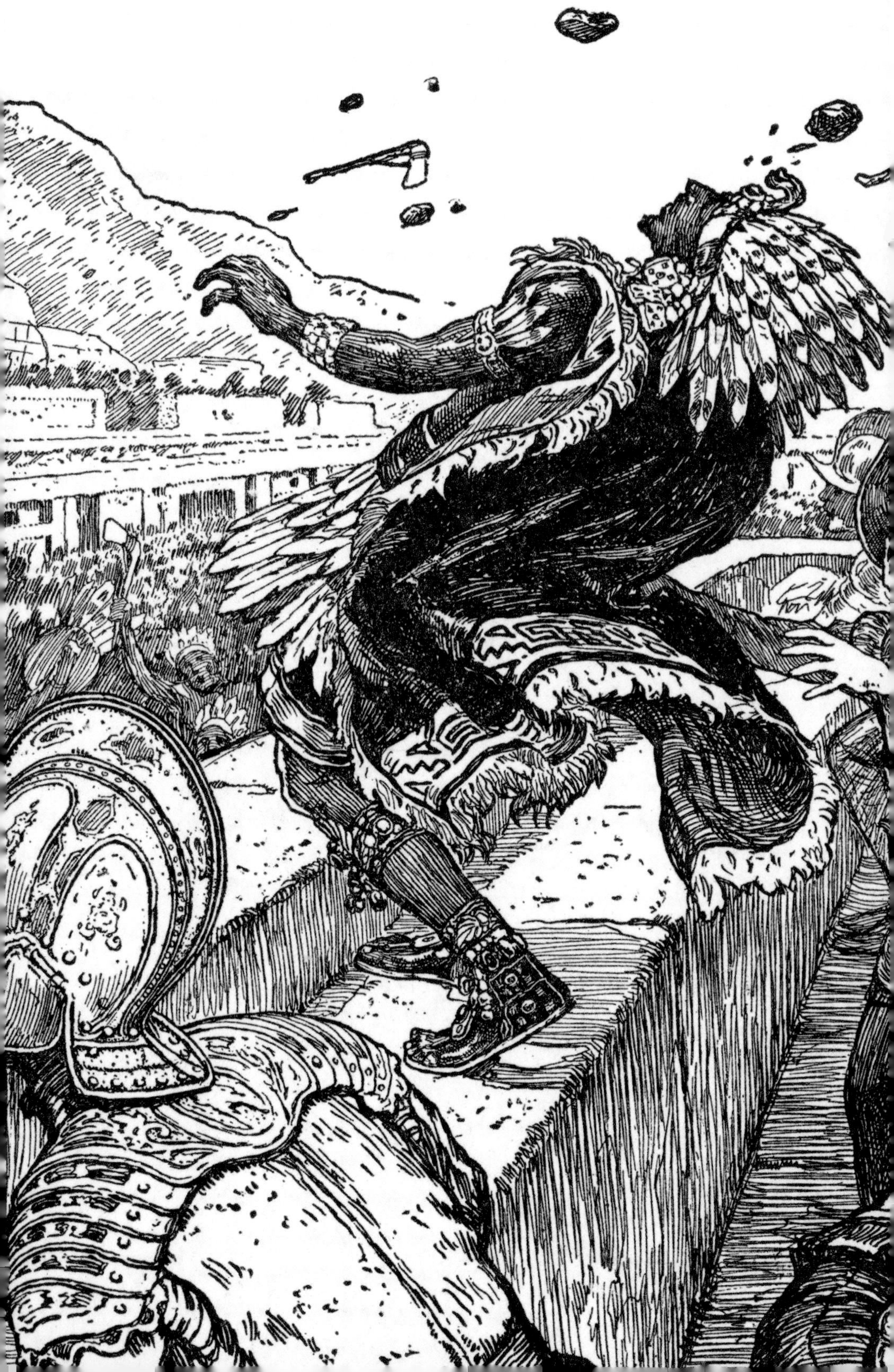

CHAPTER FOUR

The Aftermath of La Noche Triste

The night of sorrows brought victory to the Aztecs and was the first defeat Cortés experienced since arriving in Mexico. In fact, the Spanish defeat at Tenochtitlán was the biggest defeat ever experienced by any Europeans who traveled to the New World.

While the Spanish were licking their wounds, the Aztecs were left to pick up the rubble in the aftermath of battle. They started to settle their lives back to normal again and prepare for an upcoming festival. Any captive Spaniards and Tlaxcalans who had survived the night of sorrows were sacrificed. The feeling of confidence that came with defeating the Spanish was undercut by what the battle revealed about their once-strong empire. The Aztecs now realized that the subjugated tribes had no loyalty to their emperor. Aztec morale had been demoralized by a small number of conquistadors and their superior weapons. Much of their great city of Tenochtitlán had been destroyed.

Opposite: Montezuma was stoned by his own people for appeasing the Spanish invaders.

The Aztec uprising in Tenochtitlán led to the first Spanish defeat in Mexico.

The Aftermath of *La Noche Triste*

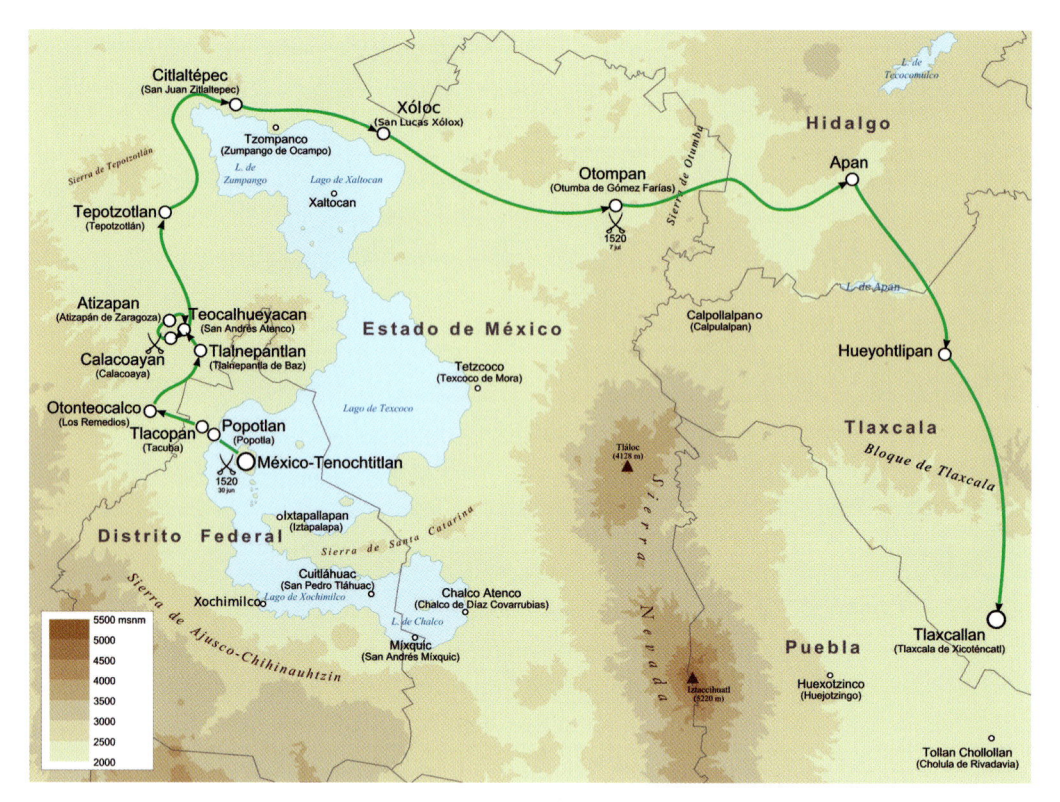

This map shows the route Cortés and his men took in retreat from Tenochtitlán after defeat.

Nevertheless, Cuitláhuac did not seem concerned about anticipating future attacks from the vanquished Spanish. Military preparations were not a priority. The battle with the Spanish revealed them to be not gods as Montezuma had believed, but rather humans, able to be killed. Perhaps this gave the Aztecs a false sense of overconfidence. Cuitláhuac made no further effort to pursue the Spanish and finish them off. He assumed, wrongly, that they had been utterly defeated. What he did not know was that Cortés, in a speech to his injured army, did not regard *la noche triste* as a defeat, merely a tactical setback.

EARLIEST KNOWN ACCOUNTS OF MONTEZUMA'S CONFLICT WITH CORTÉS

The earliest accounts of Montezuma's conflict with Hernán Cortés are from Cortés's own writings—letters to the king of Spain. Writing five letters, he offered a personal account of his conquest of Mexico (dubbed New Spain). The earliest of these letters, dated July 1519 CE, remains lost. The second, third, and fourth letters were published in Spain in the years 1522, 1523, and 1525 respectively. The fifth and final letter remained unpublished until 1842.

Cortés's second letter describes Tenochtitlán and the Aztec king Montezuma (of whom he writes admiringly). He documents their early contacts with Montezuma's emissaries, their alliance with the Tlaxcalans, their march to the capital, and ultimately meeting Montezuma in person. Cortés describes "the 'night of sorrows' in which Cortés and his men fought their way out of the city, and the events leading up to his departure from the capital."

It is important to keep in mind that while they are primary sources, these letters are one-sided versions of events between Cortés and Montezuma and the Aztec people. Codices are the next best primary sources; however, the original Aztec texts were burned by the Spanish. The codices existing today are Spanish reproductions documenting the Aztecs, Montezuma, and the conquest. Though Spanish friars worked with the conquered Aztecs to understand their culture, beliefs, and daily life for purposes of documentation, these reproductions must be viewed through a critical lens. The Codex Mendoza, reproduced by native scribes twenty years post-conquest, under supervision by Spanish priests, includes the conflicts between the conquistadors and Aztecs.

Repercussions for Past Bad Behavior

When Cuitláhuac decided it was time to seek allies against the Spanish, he made overtures to various tribes directly about joining forces, including the Tlaxcalans. Each overture was met with refusal. No one liked or trusted the Aztecs after centuries of harsh domination. Cuitláhuac was beginning to feel desperate. He offered to remit all tribute for a year from any town that killed the Spanish or expelled them from the empire. This offer was refused just as his earlier overtures.

Cortés was determined to return to Tenochtitlán and conquer the Aztecs once and for all. In addition to recovering and rebuilding his strength and military stockpiles, Cortés set about to form new alliances. Generations of Aztec oppression in the valley made it easier for Cortés to convince various tribes to join forces with him against them. Thousands of natives now supported Cortés and accepted becoming **vassals** of the king of Spain (even though they may not have understood what that meant for them).

In Tenochtitlán, Cuitláhuac continued to restore the city to its former glory. Buildings were repaired, and any missing or damaged idols were replaced in their respective temples to boost morale among the people. He continued his attempts to strengthen the Aztec empire through diplomatic and alliance-building efforts, but they proved unsuccessful. The Aztecs realized Cortés was still a threat to them.

Even so, the Aztecs had no way of knowing that Cortés was preparing to return. His time spent in the great capital city gave him insight, helping him plan how best to attack it. He understood the lay of the land, entry and exit points, terrain,

Opposite: Under order by Cortés, Spanish brigantines inflicted much damage upon the Aztecs in Tenochtitlán.

The Aftermath of *La Noche Triste*

how the Aztecs fought, and their weaknesses. Cortés also decided that instead of a major assault, he would first lay **siege** to the city to weaken the Aztecs. He charged his shipbuilder with the task of making **brigantines** that could be used to sail across the lake, bringing their cannons closer to Tenochtitlán. They would then use the cannons to blast the Aztecs into surrender.

Disease Alters the Future of the Native Populations

With all his war preparations, Cortés did not even realize he had a most potent weapon on his side—disease. Smallpox, a contagious, infectious viral disease in the New World, seems to have originated in Hispaniola in 1518. In 1519, it spread to Cuba. This disease decimated native populations that had never been exposed to it before. No exposure meant no immunity; smallpox killed indiscriminately.

It is believed that the invaders from Cuba who had arrived at Vera Cruz brought the disease with them. More specifically, it is thought that one of their porters had been infected, spreading it to the natives. "The disease spread to the family in the house where he had lodged, then from one family to another, from one town to another, from one people to another. The unfortunate Totonacs, who had made themselves Cortés's first allies, were decimated."

Smallpox reached Tenochtitlán by late October 1520, about the same time that Cortés's brigantines were being built for invasion. Because the smallpox epidemic killed the natives but spared the Spanish (who had had previous exposure to the disease in Europe), the Aztecs began to see Cortés and his men not as gods, but rather as superhumans.

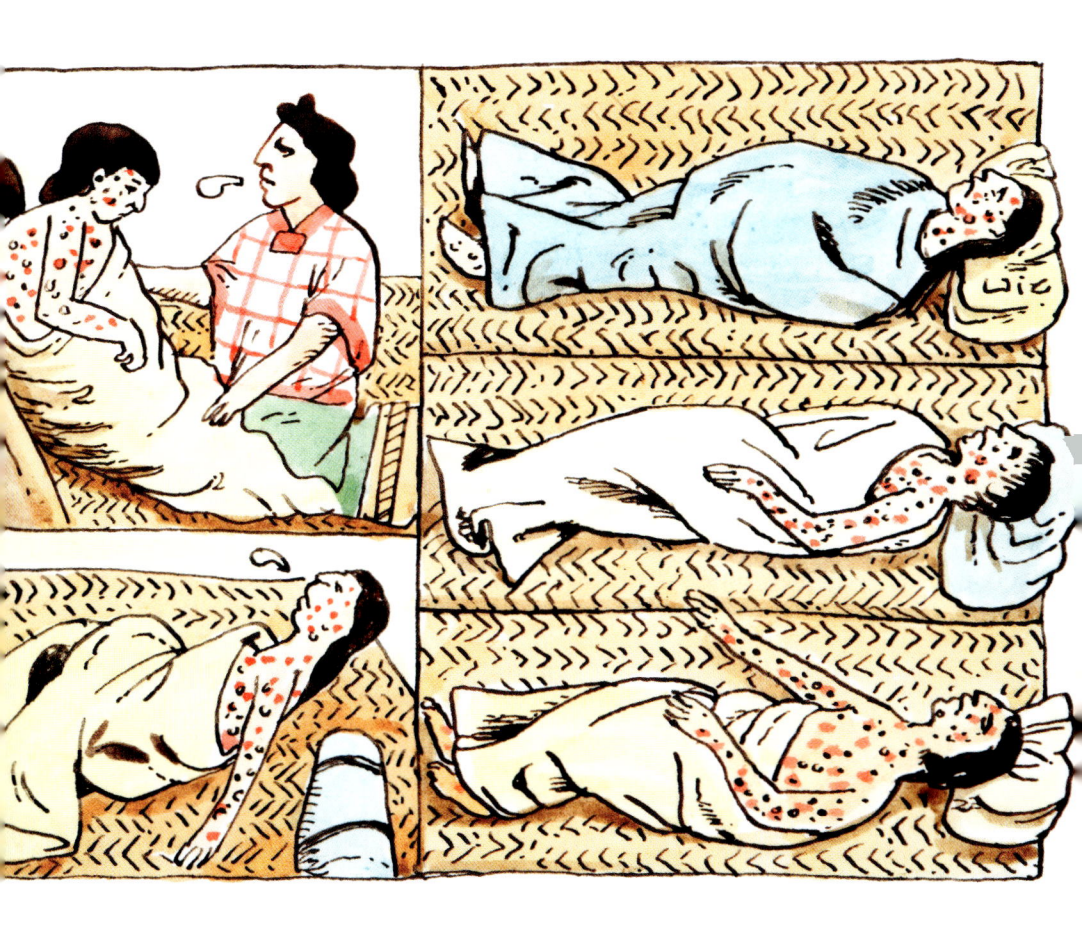

A codex depiction of the smallpox epidemic that devastated the vulnerable Aztec population

Cuitláhuac became ill with the disease and died quickly, leaving the Aztecs without an emperor for the second time in a year. The Council of Four reconvened and elected twenty-year-old Cuauhtémoc, also known as Prince Falling Eagle. He was known to be a brave fighter with a brilliant intellect. He had been a critic of Montezuma's policy of appeasement. Though he was prepared to fight the Spanish, Cuauhtémoc also followed his predecessor's

Cortés sought revenge by laying siege to
Tenochtitlán, leading to the Aztec downfall.

The Aftermath of *La Noche Triste*

attempts at alliance building. But like his predecessor, Cuauhtémoc's attempts were met with failure. He began to realize the power the Aztecs held over the tribes depended on fear, and the tribes no longer feared.

Even though they had defeated the Spanish and driven them out of Tenochtitlán, the Aztecs were poorly prepared for the impending battle Cortés was about to wage on them. They were unprepared because they lived and fought by rules and regulations. Cortés was unconventional and ruthless. He was planning to carry out a plan that was entirely unfamiliar to Aztec warfare—a European-style siege with a blockade. Cortés was not preparing for battle, but rather to put pressure on the Aztec population, weakening them by cutting off their food and water supplies.

An Unrelenting Enemy Returns

Cortés justified his impending actions by claiming the Aztecs were in rebellion, believing Montezuma had acquiesced to him and thus the king of Spain, back when they first met on the causeway of Tenochtitlán. Any action against the Spanish was an action against the Spanish crown. Putting down such rebellion was then considered a just response. Cortés also justified his actions in the name of spreading Christianity to the New World, replacing the idols, gods, and human sacrifice of the Aztecs with the "true faith." He rallied his native allies by assuring them that soon they would be free from Aztec domination.

Cortés and his newly built force headed back to Tenochtitlán, fourteen months after his first arrival there. He led his men toward Tenochtitlán, stopping in Texcoco at the end of December 1520. This was an important stop. Texcoco was a member of the Triple Alliance, and according to some historians, was at one time a senior partner in this alliance before Tenochtitlán usurped them. Cortés was unsure how he and his men would be received. To their surprise, Texcoco was empty. The conquistadors' reputation led the people to leave for safety. The Spanish raided the city's reserves and committed vandalism, including burning two palaces that contained the archives of the Texcocan and Mexican kingdoms. These archives included maps, codices, and genealogical records. Three days later, some Texcocan lords dared enter the city and requested a meeting with Cortés. They begged his forgiveness, explaining that in the past they had fought against him unwillingly under orders of the Aztecs. This time, they wanted to side with Cortés. And like that, the Triple Alliance was broken.

Cuauhtémoc soon heard of these negotiations between the Texcocans and Cortés. He urged them to side with him against the Spanish instead, but to no avail. Cortés had been well received. He offered to break the limitations on trade that had been imposed on them by Tenochtitlán. Tenochtitlán and its major market, Tlatelolco, had a monopoly on trade. This monopoly was now threatened by Cortés, making him popular among those who were tired of subjugation under the Aztecs.

Cuauhtémoc, determined not to make any concessions with Cortés, still made tactical offers to the subjugated towns for continued alliance against the Spanish. But no one wanted to align with them. In fact, the leaders of these subjugated towns were giddy at the thought of the possible fall of the Aztecs to the Spanish.

By late January 1521, Cuauhtémoc was preparing Tenochtitlán for battle with the Spanish. The city's defenses were built up, channels were deepened under the bridges, and darts and missiles were made, along with long lances to which the Aztecs planned to affix some of the swords the Spanish had left behind the year before during *la noche triste*. Meanwhile, Cortés's brigantines were almost ready for use. He had the Tlaxcalans transport them to Texcoco from the banks of the River Zahuapan just below Tlaxcala. These brigantines would be his secret weapon against the Aztecs.

Cuauhtémoc was aware of the many reconnaissance excursions that Cortés and his men took around Lake Texcoco. They met with some skirmishes but nothing significant. The Spanish either acquired more allies eager to turn against the Aztecs, or they sacked the towns. Just weeks before Cortés's siege of Tenochtitlán was to begin, Cuauhtémoc made a last attempt at diplomacy with several former subjugated cities, but they were unresponsive to his requests. They sensed the end was drawing near for the empire.

The Aztecs Make One Last Stand

Diplomacy had failed. Cuauhtémoc prepared for battle. He filled the city with soldiers and weapons but left it short on food. From his spies, he knew that Cortés was planning on using boats. In preparation, Cuauhtémoc had stakes placed under the water in the lake to impede their advance to the city. He prepared his own fleet of canoes as well. The Aztecs had used canoes in war for generations, but only for transport of warriors, not sea battle. Long, protracted war was unusual for them, let alone an amphibious siege. The Aztecs were used to battles lasting for a few days. Cuauhtémoc probably thought the Spanish would make a frontal assault on the city.

Cortés organized his forces into four divisions: three for land battle and the fourth for water battle (under his command) in the brigantines. Each brigantine bow carried a small bronze cannon. The three land divisions were ordered to hold the three main entrances to Tenochtitlán. A fourth causeway was left open to allow Aztecs to retreat from the city when the pressure of the siege got to them.

In late May 1521, the Spanish sabotaged the spring where the fresh water flowed from conduits through the aqueducts that Montezuma I had built, cutting off the water supply to Tenochtitlán. The brigantines were put into action on June 1, 1521. The Spanish siege cut off food supplies from reaching Tenochtitlán, which forced the Aztecs to rely on what reserves they had within the city. Since the city's population relied heavily on tribute from conquered tribes for food, they were not in a good position with subjugated tribes switching allegiances to Cortés. Tributes were cut off.

Skirmishes took place outside of Tenochtitlán. Cuauhtémoc, understanding the tactics of Cortés, divided his warriors into four divisions to face their Spanish counterparts. The fourth division defended against the brigantines to prevent their landing. Cuauhtémoc supervised the defensive strategy via canoe, as he was paddled from place to place. He was angry that many formerly good allies had abandoned him, and, determined not to show any weakness, he ordered women to take up fighting if their husbands died. Nearly the entire population of Tenochtitlán was to be mobilized for defense.

Some of the Spanish brigantines had succeeded in avoiding the hidden underwater stakes and paddled into the city. Once inside, they set fire to houses in the southern part of Tenochtitlán.

Initial Spanish successes on the first day of the siege were followed by weeks that were slow and painful. The Aztecs quickly adapted to dealing with new threats. Cortés controlled the lake with his brigantines. He continued finding ways to breach the city and burn homes, but his forces were always attacked by stones, arrows, and darts. The Aztecs were not short on manpower.

By mid-June, Cortés and his men breached the city and, using guns, blasted obstacles in their path. This caused the Aztecs to flee toward the square in front of the Great Temple. More gunfire allowed the Spanish to push further into the city, which made the warriors retreat into the temple enclosure. But the Aztecs turned the tables and pushed the Spanish out and back toward the causeway, bombarding them with stones from rooftops. In retreat, Cortés had his men set fire to the houses. Once the rooftops were burnt down, the Aztecs would not be able to use them as a place to launch their aerial assault again.

After several days, Cortés made another attempt to breach the city and was met with much resistance. The numbers of the Aztecs, along with their stamina and their discipline, made Cortés realize the Aztecs would fight to the death before surrendering. This meant Tenochtitlán had to be destroyed. Cortés decided to enter the city every day in the same entry point and attack different places. He then withdrew his men. This tactic enabled the Spanish to make breaches (only to be filled in by Aztecs during the night), burn houses, and cause whatever damage they could. Cortés thought Cuauhtémoc would surrender by the end of June. The Spanish had, by then, conquered half of Tenochtitlán. The Aztecs remained steadfast in their resistance even though much more hardship lay ahead of them.

The Aztec resilience was impressive. The Spaniards filled in their ditches in the causeways by day, and each night, the Aztecs re-dug them to impede their enemy. They continued to withstand attacks on three fronts, adapting to an attacking enemy who used horses, guns, and steel swords. The Aztecs inflicted much damage on the Spanish using their obsidian-edged weapons, stones, arrows, war clubs, and even sticks.

The tide turned against the Spanish on June 30, 1521, when many were captured and sacrificed for all to witness. The sacrifices horrified the Spanish and also concerned the various native tribes who had chosen to align themselves with Cortés against the Aztecs. Were they about to experience an Aztec revival of strength? Had they chosen the wrong alliance? But food and water ran low for the Aztecs, and the city remained blockaded. By mid-July, Cortés believed the fierce resistance on June 30 had been the Aztecs' last stand.

Tlaxcalans launched an attack into the city without the Spanish. They raided and battled the Aztecs, who pushed them back. The Tlaxcalans took captives before retreating at nightfall. This had a powerful and positive psychological impact on the Spanish and their native allies. The Aztecs showed signs of fatigue due to the food shortages and inadequate water supply. They had lost many men, too.

The Spanish breached the city, arrived at the spring that had been providing the Aztecs with a modest amount of water, and destroyed it. The only water left for the Aztecs was from the lake, and it was unsanitary. Many died from drinking it. While the Aztecs got weaker, Cortés and his men got stronger with the arrival of more gunpowder, crossbows, and reinforcements from Vera Cruz. A ship that was part of Spaniard Ponce de Léon's expedition to Florida (to establish a Spanish colony) had landed on the coast at just the right moment in the Spanish siege of Tenochtitlán.

The siege and skirmishes continued for another month. By August 12, 1521, Cuauhtémoc finally recognized that their defeat was imminent. However, he couldn't bring himself to surrender and negotiate peace. Surrender went against his training. Cuauhtémoc most likely thought the gods would intervene, saving him and the Aztec empire.

The siege was nearing eighty days. Cuauhtémoc could still not surrender, so he prepared to secretly leave Tenochtitlán by canoe. Whether he had decided to flee to save himself or to seek new ground in a last futile attempt to keep the Aztec resistance alive is unclear. The next morning, Cortés entered Tenochtitlán. Everyone was ordered to look for Cuauhtémoc.

Aztec citizens eager to escape the war-torn city were viciously murdered by the Tlaxcalans—against Cortés's orders. One of the brigantine commanders spotted a canoe with a "person of rank" in it. He gave chase as the canoe made its way across the lake away from the destroyed city. The commander ordered the canoe to stop, but initially, it did not. Cuauhtémoc was indeed the person of rank inside. He finally realized that the Spanish outnumbered him. It was finally time to surrender. He was brought before Cortés, who received him as an emperor. He was impressed by Cuauhtémoc's courage and defense of Tenochtitlán.

After eighty days, the glorious city of Tenochtitlán, heart of the Aztec empire, had finally fallen to the Spanish a year after Montezuma's death. The city was reduced to rubble, which clogged the canals, with thousands of bodies mixed in. Cortés feared plague. He ordered his soldiers to burn what remained of the ruins. He also ordered the remaining Aztec warriors and civilians to abandon the city. The destruction and loss of

Tenochtitlán was a great tragedy, for it was more than the loss of just a city; an entire civilization was now gone.

Aztec Civilization Is Changed Forever

For the citizens of Tenochtitlán, the aftermath of the war did not provide peace. The days immediately following the fall were horrible. The Tlaxcalans, the Texcocans, and other allies roamed the city, killing indiscriminately. Bodies were everywhere, and food and water were scarce. Cuauhtémoc, while in captivity, asked Cortés to allow the surviving Aztecs to leave for neighboring towns. Cortés gave his approval, and soon the causeways leaving Tenochtitlán became full of hungry, dirty, and sick Aztec refugees who left everything behind while Tenochtitlán burned and rotted away. No one knew what would replace it. The surviving Aztecs had no hope and they had no gods.

Within a year after the destruction of Tenochtitlán and the defeat of the Aztecs, Cortés had assumed the role of de facto emperor of the former empire. During this period, the conquistadors focused on recovering from the siege and war. Reconstruction took place, and the Spanish pursuit of gold heated up. They were relentless in this quest. The old Aztec religion was replaced with Christianity, and Spanish colonization of conquered Mexico began.

Cortés decided to send some of his men out to found new settlements in the conquered territories. The conquistadors, with the help of native allies, continued their domination and pacification of outlying provinces. These provinces soon fell under the new dominion called New Spain. By 1522, Cortés returned his focus to Tenochtitlán.

By conquering Tenochtitlán, Cortés had conquered Mexico. What would happen now? A new city, Mexico City, would be built on the ruins of the old Aztec capital. Cortés drew up plans for the city. They followed the street lines and waterways of Tenochtitlán. Lots were marked for buildings: cathedral, prison, governor's palace, markets, monasteries, etc. Mexico City was to be a classic city.

Cortés built his own palace on the site of Montezuma's former palace. Native artisans and non-noble Aztecs helped construct the new city. Carvings and decorations were the work of these artisans. The great pyramid remained in place for another generation before it was blown up, ridding the city of a symbol of a horrific past. Today, one can see just a corner of the old temple, which archaeologists excavated from rubble.

The Aztecs easily adapted to the European way of doing things as the reconstruction continued over the years. They learned how to use wheels for transportation, such as on carts, instead of only using them for children's toys. The use of mules was also a great improvement on transportation. The Aztecs embraced European techniques. Even Nahuatl and other native languages began to integrate with Latin. The Spanish friars hoped they would eagerly adapt to their newly imposed Christian religion.

Yet, for all the acceptance of and transition into their new life, the Aztecs faced hardships. Morale was low not only for them but for other tribes in the valley. Many Aztecs were enslaved, and others were forced laborers. Their leaders were executed, and their native monuments, sculptures, and books were destroyed. Only pottery was left undestroyed. Possessing pottery was not considered idolatrous. Besides a loss of freedom and culture, the conquered Aztecs lost much more.

The dark side of the Spanish conquest for the Aztecs and other native peoples was that it unleashed diseases from Europe that the indigenous population had no immunity against. Not just smallpox, but influenza, whooping cough, and the mumps wreaked havoc on the natives, decimating towns and villages across Mexico. Spanish estimates of the native population in 1518 as 8 million shows a decline to 2.6 million people just forty-two years later in 1560.

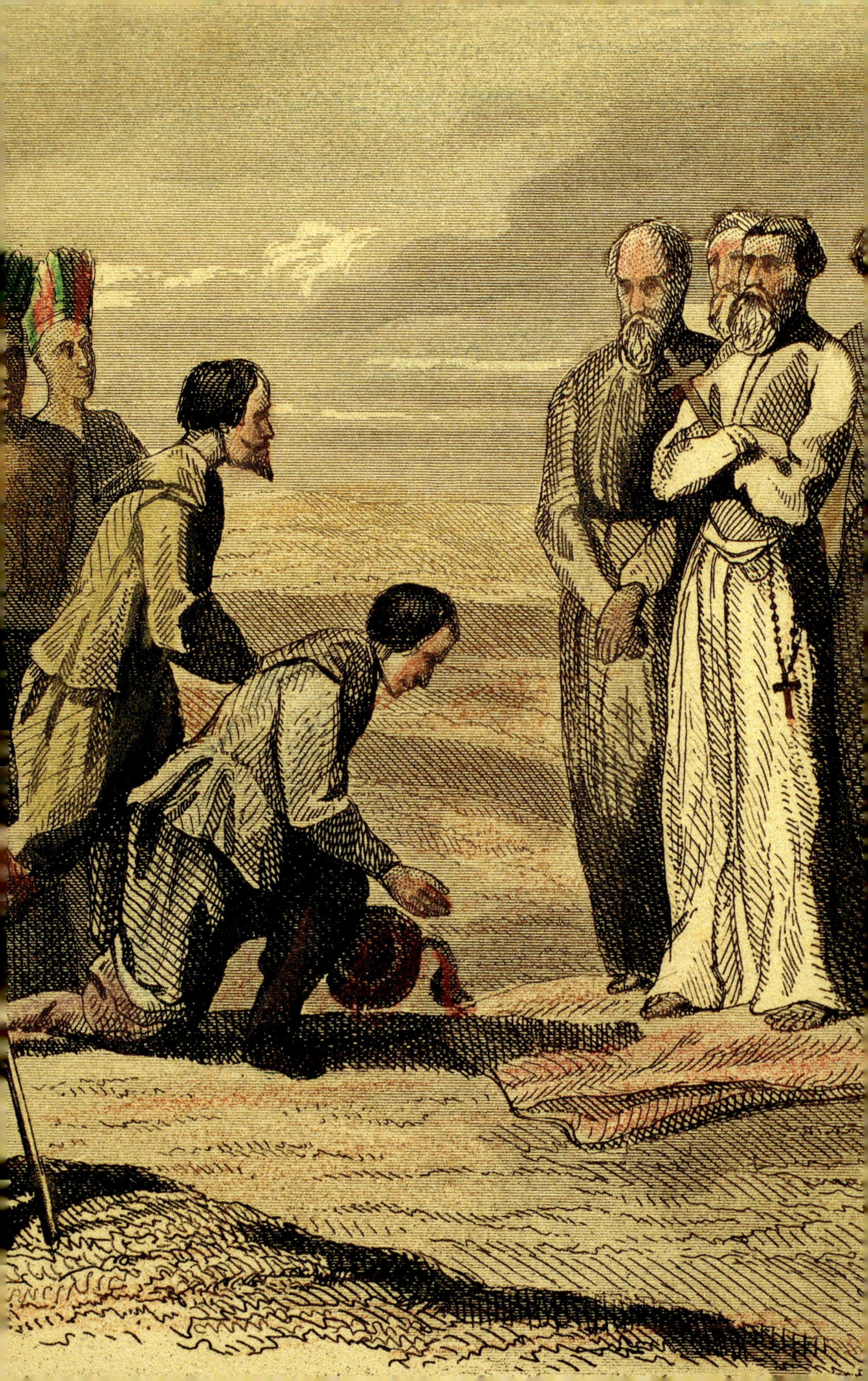

CHAPTER FIVE

Myths, Legends, *and* Popular Culture

Most perceptions of Montezuma are filtered through a Western lens, mainly a Spanish one. After Cortés conquered the Aztecs, the Spanish destroyed Aztec documents, records, and works of art. It was important to them to stamp out evidence of their culture prior to imposing a new, Spanish culture onto the surviving people. Over time, Aztec religion, customs, and culture changed as Spanish religion and customs were introduced into society. Much of what is known about the Aztecs comes from Spanish documentation, which itself is based on their observations of this conquered people and Aztec books that were translated into Spanish.

Changing Perceptions

While Spanish Christian missionaries were determined to eradicate the pagan Aztec religion and thus many aspects of

Opposite: Spanish friars spread Christianity in Mexico by converting Aztecs from their old religion.

daily Aztec life that revolved around their religion, some friars managed to preserve knowledge about the Aztecs pre-conquest. It is from their work, albeit through a Spanish filter, that we have information about the Aztecs, their religion, culture, leaders, and ultimate defeat to the Spanish.

Though there are many codices in existence that relate to the Aztecs, pre- and post-conquest Mexico, and other tribes, one document in particular is the most comprehensive record of information about Aztec daily life: the Florentine Codex. Historian Hugh Thomas has indicated that the consultants for this codex were all Mexicans (Aztec) and former students of the calmécac. These men would have learned Aztec songs, legends, and speeches by heart. Thomas considers this codex the greatest source on old Mexico.

The Florentine Codex is a set of twelve books. These books describe Aztec life pre-conquest. Franciscan friar Bernardino de Sahagún oversaw the creation of this codex between 1540 and 1585. Conversations and interviews with the indigenous people in Tlatelolco, Texcoco, and Tenochtitlán provide the details of the depictions of Aztec life. Written in Nahuatl by Aztec students of Sahagún, the codex includes roughly 1,800 illustrations by Aztecs using European techniques. A Spanish version also exists and is known as the *Historia General de las Cosas de Nueva España*. The codex is much like an encyclopedia. Content is divided into categories by subject matter. Some of these subjects include Aztec history, major gods, calendar, social structure, and perceptions of the natural world.

By documenting Aztec life, Sahagún became a pioneer in the field of ethnography before the field really existed. His writings are valuable to anyone studying the Aztec empire, pre- and post-conquest. However, as German philosopher Walter Benjamin stated, "All human knowledge takes the form

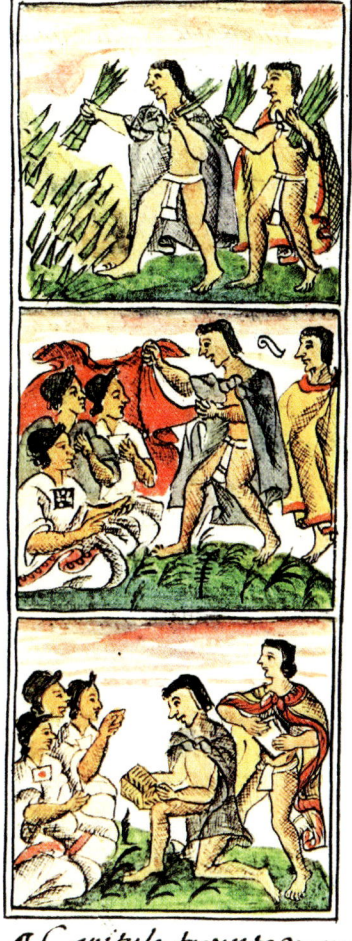

This is one example of the representative depictions and texts found in the Florentine Codex.

of interpretation." Therefore, many resources written about Montezuma are colored by the interpretation of secondhand source materials. After all, with Spanish destruction of original

Myths, Legends, and Popular Culture

Montezuma has continued to appear in pop culture, such as a character in this comic book from 1972.

102 Montezuma II

MONTEZUMA LIVES ON

People may only be familiar with Montezuma through popular culture references such as a roller coaster ride at an amusement park that bears his name, an episode of a Scooby-Doo cartoon mystery, a Hanna-Barbera comic book, or the title of a song by American indie folk band Fleet Foxes.

There is a familiarity with Montezuma that comes through pop culture, myths, and legends. Yet this familiarity does not mean that he is really known. None of these references illustrate Montezuma as an individual, a great warrior, a high priest, or as the deeply spiritual person he was. Such references boil the man down, distilling him until all that is left are small bits of knowledge: he was an Aztec emperor, he had a great empire and lots of gold, and he lost his empire to the Spanish. These bits do not give us any pertinent information about Montezuma, but they can be used as a gateway into history. Following these bits of information through the past can give a more well-rounded perspective of Montezuma as a great leader whose decisions made in response to highly unusual circumstances led to the loss of both his life and the Aztec civilization.

Aztec documentation of their own culture, no original primary source materials exist.

Perspectives about Montezuma seem to change depending on whether he or Cortés are the subjects of the material. For example, one researcher provides a more well-rounded view of Montezuma, helping to give the perspective of the leader as a person. However, another researcher presents Montezuma as weak, and the material is slanted toward Cortés. The author of the material portrays Montezuma in a more two-dimensional manner. Yes, Montezuma's choices, actions, or lack of actions ultimately led to the beginning of the end of the Aztec empire. However, understanding Montezuma as a complex individual guided by deep faith and belief in portents, fate, and prophecies should be considered a factor in his decision-making process when confronted with a situation before unknown to the Aztecs. No other Aztec emperor was faced with such a situation when considering what to do about the Spanish. It is unknown how they would have responded—perhaps the same as Montezuma?

As recently as 2009, the British Museum curated a special exhibit that reexamined the life of Montezuma. Their goal was to present the story of Montezuma from an Aztec perspective, reinforcing the fact that what people know about him already might be based on Spanish versions of history, i.e., "history written by the victors."

"A lot of the perceptions of Montezuma and these tumultuous events of the Spanish Conquest are seen through a Western lens," said curator Colin MacEwan. "The challenge is to try to tell the side of the story that isn't usually told. It's personalizing history and establishing a more direct connection with one person's footprint in history." According to MacEwan, Montezuma was much more complicated and skilled than is generally recognized.

Presenting the doomed Aztec emperor in this manner has been important for a contemporary audience. It reminds us that history and historical figures should be approached from multiple sources and perspectives. There are always two sides to every story (and sometimes even more). People and events are not one-dimensional. And most importantly, history can easily be modified or erased to suit the purposes of the victors. The irony, where Montezuma is concerned, is that the Aztecs did to Toltec history what the Spanish did to the Aztecs: destroyed it and rewrote it to suit their own perspective.

Similar actions still take place in the modern world: the Nazis burned books in Germany in 1933, the Taliban destroyed pre-Islamic religious artifacts in Afghanistan in 2001, the Islamic State of Iraq and Syria (ISIS) destroyed an ancient temple representing Greco-Roman and Persian influences in Syria in 2015. Conquerors seek to destroy the important texts, artifacts, and religion of those they conquer, substituting everything with their own versions. Only when looking at a wide array of historical materials from a variety of sources can people begin to piece together a more multifaceted version of a historical figure, event, or time period.

The impact of this special exhibit on Montezuma by the British Museum is that it changed his story that had been told from a European presentation and restored him to that which he was: the last great emperor of a vast empire. In the process, Aztec power and might were also restored and appreciated in a new light.

How Montezuma is viewed and thought of is highly important to the Mexican people. In looking back on their own history, their perspective of this Aztec emperor is conflicted. He was considered a tyrant by some, and one whose judgment was called into question. His tactical decisions against the Spanish invaders were seen, in hindsight, as disastrous. As compared to prior Aztec leaders, Montezuma's greatness is diminished; he is looked back upon as weak and vacillating instead of defiant and in control.

Miguel Baez of Mexico's National Institute of Anthropology and History acknowledges that Montezuma's image is ambiguous. "He was a great emperor who consolidated the Mexican empire, but he is also seen as the guy who lost against the Spanish, and I don't believe any culture likes a loser."

Myths and Legends of Montezuma

When looking back on ancient times, contemporary researchers, historians, anthropologists, and ethnographers must piece together history. Often the only clues to how people lived, events of their time, and their leaders are discovered through tangible artifacts or oral history. Oral history, coming initially from primary sources, is at risk for misinterpretation or misrepresentation. Much like the childhood game of "telephone," information can get distorted. Legends and myths perpetuate information that may, at one time, been rooted in fact but over time has evolved into unauthenticated stories.

In the southwestern United States, some Native American tribes such as the Tohono O'odham and the Pueblo share a hero-god in mythology named Montezuma. References to this hero-god imply that the tribes share a belief that Montezuma's name is that of a great king and that he once ruled over a vast empire that included Mexico. They believe he is buried inside an Arizona mountain that bears his image. According to Tohono O'odham tribal myth, the Great Spirit discovers clay when digging a hole. He drops the clay into the hole again, and Montezuma emerges.

Montezuma then assists the Great Spirit in bringing all the native tribes out of the hole.

Offshoot stories of this myth include some similar to the Christian stories of the Tower of Babel and Noah and the Great Flood. Another tale claims Montezuma's control over the various tribes led men to become evil, hunting and killing. When the Great Spirit's warnings to stop their evil ways went unheeded, he punished the tribes with winter (snow, ice, and hail) and he even brought the Spanish to fight anyone who opposed him.

When it comes to legends surrounding Montezuma, many persist concerning what happened to all his gold. The Spanish were greedy for gold, valuing it in a different way than did the Aztecs. Montezuma's emissaries presented Cortés with gifts that contained gold, which he then had melted down into gold bricks for transport to Spain. Meant to satisfy the Spanish as a tribute to persuade them to leave the shores of Mexico, the gifts of gold only encouraged them to stay for more.

Montezuma gave Cortés gold willingly, though he was baffled by the Spanish desire for something the Aztecs did not consider important. *Teocuitlatl*, the Nahuatl word for gold, literally means "excrement of the gods." Once inside Tenochtitlán, the Spanish began amassing gold from the Aztecs. Cortés sent some directly to the king of Spain and kept much of the rest for himself. His conquistadors were given gold as well for payment of their services. However, much of the gold the Spanish acquired for removal from the Aztec capital never made it out as planned on the night of sorrows.

As Cortés and his men attempted to escape Tenochtitlán on *la noche triste*, those carrying gold with them were either slowed by their load and killed, or they drowned in the canals and Lake Texcoco from the weight of the gold. Much of the gold was lost in the water. This lost gold came to be known as Montezuma's

Cortés received gifts of gold from Montezuma, which enticed him to stay in Mexico longer.

Treasure, and numerous legends have emerged surrounding it. Today, the only thing that is certain is that Montezuma's Treasure has never been found. Many theories have been put forth as to the gold's final resting place.

The most popular theory is that Montezuma's gold remains exactly where it was dropped, at the bottom of Lake Texcoco. Many treasure hunters, including a former Mexican president, have searched the lake but to no avail. Another theory claims that the Spaniards retrieved the treasure when they returned to Tenochtitlán, but the ship that carried the gold back to Spain sank in a storm at sea. A more intriguing theory places the treasure up north in Utah.

In 1914, a man by the name of Freddy Crystal showed up in Kanab, Utah, with a map he claimed gave the location of

Montezuma's gold. Crystal was a miner and amateur treasure hunter, and he said he had come across the map while in an old Mexico City church that was awaiting demolition. The map had been tucked away inside an old manuscript; the manuscript had been written by a Spanish friar in Tenochtitlán at the time of the Spanish conquest. It was believed the information on the map was gathered through the torture of one of the Aztec porters who delivered Montezuma's Treasure to its hidden location. Crystal made the connection between the map and the geography of southern Utah. Having spent time in Utah a few years earlier, Crystal had been trying to understand Aztec petroglyphs that he found on canyon walls. Making the connection between the Utah canyons and what the map depicted, Crystal felt certain Montezuma's Treasure was hidden somewhere near Kanab.

Crystal had located sealed tunnels in Johnson's Canyon by 1920, but no treasure was ever found. Even so, treasure hunters to this day are still looking for it in Utah. It is thought that the tunnels in Johnson Canyon are decoys, and that the real treasure lies in caverns hidden at the base of a pond, 36 feet (11 m) below the surface. Divers have attempted to locate the treasure, but these dives were cut short due to disorientation underwater and strange claims of seeing ghosts of Aztec warriors.

But was Montezuma's gold really carried this far north and hidden, or had he truly given it all to the Spanish? Is it possible some of the gold still exists beneath the surface of modern-day Mexico City, formerly Tenochtitlán? In 1981, a gold bar weighing in at 4 pounds (2 kilograms) was found in mud 15 feet (4.5 m) below street level on a building site. Mexican archaeologists believed it to be the only remnant of Montezuma's Treasure to be found in Mexico City. This gold bar was unearthed in a location consistent with the site of a canal along a causeway in 1521. Upon examination, the gold bar contained 93.98 percent gold, 5.24 percent copper, and 0.78 percent iron. This mixture of gold, copper, and iron is indicative of the conquistadors' rushed foundry process to melt down gold for easier transport, as described in the memoirs of one of Cortés's captains.

"There are all sorts of myths about the treasure of Montezuma, but Cortés got all there was," according to Gaston Garcia Cantu, director of Mexico's Anthropology and History Institute. "There is no evidence to suggest that there is a treasure hidden or lost somewhere."

Montezuma Permeates Pop Culture

People have been fascinated with Montezuma for centuries. In 2002, the opera *Montezuma*, which was written in 1733, was discovered in an archive of a music library in Berlin, Germany. Penned by the Italian Baroque composer, Antonio Vivaldi, this opera made its premiere in Venice on November 14, 1733, and was thought to have been lost. It was one of the earliest operas written based on the "New World." Exotic stories set in distant lands were all the rage in eighteenth-century Europe.

References to Montezuma can be heard in the official hymn of the United State Marine Corps, which opens with the phrase, "From the halls of Montezuma." This references when the Marines took part in the Battle of Chapultepec in Mexico City during the Mexican-American War (1846–1848). Archeologists have confirmed the first identified culture in Chapultepec to be that of the Toltecs. They gave the area its name, Chapultepec, which means "grasshopper hill" in Nahuatl. Remains of a Toltec altar have been found on the hill's summit. *Halls of Montezuma*

Montezuma Castle National Monument in Arizona is an architectural artifact from prehistoric times.

is also the name of a 1951 World War II film about US Marines fighting on a Japanese-held island.

When planning your family's next road trip to the US Southwest, consider stopping off at Montezuma Castle National Monument, located in Camp Verde, Arizona. The name is misleading since the dwellings were not built by Montezuma, nor are they a castle, but rather a prehistoric high-rise apartment. These ruins, first discovered in 1860 by European Americans, were mistakenly thought to be Aztec creations, made at the order of Montezuma, so they were dubbed Montezuma Castle. In actuality, these ruins had been built and used by the Sinagua people (pre-Columbian) from 1100 to 1425. These people abandoned the dwellings forty years before Montezuma's birth.

If you find yourself wondering what it was like to be Montezuma and rule the great Aztec empire, modern technology gives you the opportunity to see for yourself in the video game *Civilization VI*.

Lastly, "Montezuma's Revenge" is not only a thrilling roller coaster ride at Knott's Berry Farm amusement park in California but also the humorously colloquial term for "traveler's diarrhea."

Whether Montezuma appears in myths, legends, or popular culture, one thing is clear: the man left a lasting imprint on our world long after his downfall and demise. Such references to Montezuma should trigger curiosity, leading one to follow the breadcrumbs through the ancient past to the discovery of a great and complex military leader and emperor.

CHRONOLOGY

1100 The Aztecs (Mexica) travel from their believed northern homeland Aztlan (southwestern United States)

1248 Aztecs settle near Lake Texcoco in the central valley of Mexico; Tepanecs drive them out

1325 The Aztecs found their city Tenochtitlán and settle

1350 The Aztecs build causeways with canals in and around Tenochtitlán

1370 Death of Tenoch, religious ruler of the Aztecs

1376 Acamapichitli, the first ruler of Tenochtitlán, takes the throne and rules for nineteen years

1395 Huitzilihuitzli, second ruler of Tenochtitlán, takes the throne and rules for twenty-two years

1417 Chimalpopoca, third ruler of Tenochtitlán, takes the throne and rules for ten years

1427 Aztecs war with the Tepaneca, the dominant tribe ruling central Mexico

1430 Aztecs conquer the Tepaneca

1431 The Triple Alliance is established between Tenochtitlán, Texcoco, and Tlacopan

1427 Itzcoatl, the fourth ruler of Tenochtitlán, takes the throne and rules for thirteen years

1440 Montezuma I, the fifth ruler of Tenochtitlán, takes the throne and rules for twenty-nine years

1452 Tenochtitlán suffers great damage from massive flooding

1452 Tenochtitlán suffers a famine for two years

1467 Montezuma II is born; son of future ruler Axayacatl; great-grandson of Montezuma I

1469 Axayacatl, the sixth ruler of Tenochtitlán, takes the throne and rules for twelve years

1481 Tizoc, the seventh ruler of Tenochtitlán, takes the throne and rules for five years

1486 Ahuitzotl, eighth ruler of Tenochtitlán, takes the throne and rules for sixteen years

1487 Dedication of the Great Temple at Tenochtitlán, the sixth version of the temple

1502 Montezuma II, the ninth ruler of Tenochtitlán, takes the throne and rules for eighteen years

1517 Appearance of a comet, which is seen as an omen of impending doom

1519 Spaniard Hernán Cortés lands on the Yucatan Peninsula on March 4

1519 Cortés finally arrives in Tenochtitlán and meets Montezuma II on November 8

1520 Cortés leaves Tenochtitlán and returns to eastern shore to face Spanish invaders (late May)

1520 In Cortés's absence, his conquistadors massacre the Aztecs in Tenochtitlán (late June)

1520 Aztec uprising ensues; Montezuma II is stoned by his people and dies (late June)

1520 The Spanish massacred by Aztecs in *la noche triste* on July 1

1520 Cuitahuac, tenth ruler of Tenochtitlán, takes the throne, dies of smallpox in two months

1520 Cuauhtémoc, eleventh and last ruler of Tenochtitlán, takes the throne and rules for one year

1521 Fall of Tenochtitlán after eighty-day siege by the Spanish; end of the Aztec empire

1522 Cortés rebuilds Tenochtitlán; capital renamed as Mexico City

1525 Cuauhtémoc is hanged by the Spaniards

GLOSSARY

ANAHUAC The Nahuatl name for Mexico.

AQUEDUCT An artificial channel for conveying water.

BRIGANTINE A two-masted sailing ship; also known as a schooner.

CALMÉCAC The temple school that prepared Aztec boys to become priests or for high state office.

CAUSEWAY A raised road or track across low or wet ground.

CHINAMPA Floating gardens; intensely cultivated artificial garden islands that remained fertile through drought.

CODEX An ancient manuscript or book made of a long, narrow strip of paper folded like a fan; plural form is "codices."

CONQUISTADOR A conqueror, especially one of the Spanish conquerors of Mexico and Peru.

COUNCIL OF FOUR The top advisors to the ruling Aztec emperor, usually military generals, who also elected the emperors; also known as the Great Council.

DIVINATORY Attempting to discover the future or outcome of future events via supernatural means.

FATE The development of events beyond a person's control determined by a supernatural power.

GARLAND WARS Predetermined ritual wars between the Aztecs and neighboring tribes to obtain prisoners for sacrifice and tribute; also known as Flower Wars.

GLYPH A hieroglyphic character or symbol; a pictograph.

HARQUEBUSIER A soldier armed with a harquebus, an early type of portable gun supported on a tripod.

HUITZILOPOCHTLI Aztec god of the sun and war; patron god of the Aztecs; name means Hummingbird-on-the-Left.

LACUSTRINE Of, relating to, or associated with lakes.

MEXICA The term the Aztecs used to refer to themselves (they did not call themselves Aztecs).

NAHUATL The native language spoken by the Aztecs and other Nahua tribes.

OBSIDIAN A dark, volcanic glass used for making tools, blades, and spear points.

OCELOT A South American spotted leopard-like cat.

OMEN An event regarded as a portent of good or evil; event of prophetic significance.

POCHTECATL Professional, long-distance traveling Aztec merchants; sometimes doubled as spies for the Aztec emperors.

PORTENT A sign or warning that something momentous or calamitous is about to happen.

PROPHECY A prediction of future events.

QUETZALCOATL Chief Toltec and Aztec god identified with the wind and air, represented by a feathered serpent.

SACRIFICE The slaughtering an animal or person as an offering to a god or supernatural figure.

SIEGE A military operation in which enemy forces surround a town, cutting off essential supplies, to force the surrender of those inside.

SUBJUGATE To conquer, bringing under complete control.

TELPOCHCALLI The military school for Aztec boys in which to learn fighting and strategy.

TENOCHTITLÁN The capital city of the Aztec empire, means "cactus rock" in Nahuatl.

TEPUZTLI Nahuatl word for copper.

TLALOC Aztec god of water and rain.

TOLTECS The Pre-Aztec civilization whom the Aztecs claimed to be descended from.

TONALPOHUALLI Aztec sacred calendar (260 days) focused on rituals of the gods; divinatory tool; book of fate.

TONALPOUHQUE Nahuatl word for astrologer.

TRIBUTE The Aztec form of annual tax collection from subjugated tribes, paid in materials, food, and prisoners for sacrifice.

TRIPLE ALLIANCE A political and military alliance between the three Nahua city-states Tenochtitlán, Texcoco, and Tlacopan that formed the backbone of the Aztec empire; Tenochtitlán quickly became the most dominant.

VASSAL A person who promises loyalty to a leader in return for protection from that leader.

VERA CRUZ Territory on eastern shore of Aztec empire (now a state in Mexico) at which the Spanish arrived and created the first Spanish settlement called Villa Rica de la Vera Cruz on May 18, 1519.

XIUHPOHUALLI Aztec agriculture calendar (365 days) of rituals focused on seasonal agriculture.

FURTHER INFORMATION

BOOKS

Apte, Sunita. *The Aztec Empire*. True Books: Ancient Civilizations. New York: Scholastic, 2010.

Baquedano, Elizabeth. *Eyewitness Aztec, Inca, Maya*. DK Eyewitness. New York: DK, 2011.

Coe, Michael D., and Rex Koontz. *Mexico: From Olmecs to the Aztecs. Ancient Peoples and Places*. 7th Edition. London, UK: Thames & Hudson, 2013.

Green, Carl R. *Cortés: Conquering the Powerful Aztec Empire*. Great Explorers of the World. New York: Enslow Publishers, 2010.

Tsouras, Peter G. *Warlords of Ancient Mexico: How the Mayans and Aztecs Ruled for More Than a Thousand Years*. New York: Skyhorse Publishing, 2014.

VIDEOS

Mocuhtezoma and the Coming of Cortés

https://www.youtube.com/watch?v=x_DGOQpQVVw
This short video documents the arrival of Cortés and Montezuma.

Prophecy of Quexalcote

http://www.history.com/topics/aztecs/videos/prophecy-of-quexalcote?m=528e394da93ae&s=undefined&f=1&free=false
This short video explores the prophecy of Quetzalcoatl and ultimately Cortés.

Tenochtitlán AZTEC EMPIRE | HISTORY of AZTECS

https://www.youtube.com/watch?v=6o7ZIHfte_k
This is a brief documentary about the city of Tenochtitlán.

Tenochtitlan (The Impossible City)

https://www.youtube.com/watch?v=_nS6MpVbB_g
Here is a brief history of the ancient Aztec capital city of Tenochtitlán.

What Happened to the Aztecs?

http://www.history.com/topics/aztecs/videos
This short video discusses the fall of the mighty Aztec empire.

WEBSITES

Ancient History Encylcopedia

http://www.ancient.eu/Montezuma
Learn more about Montezuma II in this online history encyclopedia.

Biography

http://www.biography.com/people/montezuma-ii-9412612
Read the Biography.com entry about Montezuma II here.

Encyclopedia Britannica: Montezuma II

https://www.britannica.com/biography/Montezuma-II
Explore more about Montezuma II on this online version of the *Encyclopedia Britannica*.

History: Aztecs

http://www.history.com/topics/aztecs
The History Channel's answer to the question "What Happened to the Aztecs?"

BIBLIOGRAPHY

"Aztec Civilisation." Aztecsandtenochtitlan.com. Accessed December 16, 2016. http://aztecsandtenochtitlan.com/aztec-civilisation.

Barroqueiro, Silvério A. "The Aztecs: A Pre-Columbian History." Teachersinstitute.yale.edu. Accessed December 18, 2016. http://teachersinstitute.yale.edu/curriculum/units/1999/2/99.02.01.x.html.

Burland, C.A. *Montezuma: Lord of The Aztecs*. New York: G.P. Putnam's Sons, 1973.

Burland, Cottie. *See Inside: An Aztec Town*. London, UK: Franklin Watts, 1980.

Burns, C.M. "Montezuma's Gold." Allthingsadventure.com. September 15, 2008. http://www.allthingsadventure.com/montezumas-gold.

Colonial and Aztec Codex Facsimiles. University of Arizona Library Special Collections. Accessed December 26, 2016. http://www.library.arizona.edu/exhibits/mexcodex/aztec.htm.

"Florentine Codex." Quetzal.asu.edu. Accessed December 24, 2016. http://quetzal.asu.edu/Quetzal/Culture/FlorCod.html.

Helly, Mathilde. *Montezuma and the Aztecs*. New York: Henry Holt and Company, 1996.

Jovinelly, Joann, and Jason Netelkos. *Crafts of the Ancient World: The Crafts and Culture of the Aztecs*. New York: The Rosen Publishing Group, Inc. 2003.

Katz, Gregory. "British Museum Exhibit Gives Montezuma a Little Revenge." Desertnews.com. Accessed September 27, 2009. http://www.deseretnews.com/article/705332449/British-Museum-exhibit-gives-Montezuma-a-little-revenge.html?pg=all.

Maestri, Nicoletta. "Nahuatl: The Language of the Aztec/Mexica." Archaeology.about.com. Accessed December 18, 2016. http://archaeology.about.com/od/nterms/a/Nahuatl.htm.

"Montezuma II." tenochtitlanfacts.com. Accessed December 16, 2016. http://www.tenochtitlanfacts.com/Montezuma-II.html.

"Montezuma (Mythology)." Newworldencyclopedia.org. Accessed December 24, 2016. http://www.newworldencyclopedia.org/entry/Montezuma_(mythology).

"Montezuma's Revenge." Urbandictionary.com. Accessed December 26, 2016. http://www.urbandictionary.com/define.php?term=Montezuma%27s%20revenge.

"Narrative Letter by Hernán Cortés." World Digital Library.org. Library of Congress. Accessed December 26, 2016. https://www.wdl.org/en/item/7335.

Neale, Greg. "Moctezuma: the leader who lost an empire." Telegraph.co.uk. Accessed December 24, 2016. http://www.telegraph.co.uk/culture/art/art-features/6213665/Moctezuma-the-leader-who-lost-an-empire.html.

Odijk, Pamela. *The Ancient World: The Aztecs*. South Melbourne, Australia. 1989.

Riding, Alan. "Gold Bar Found in Mexico Thought to be Cortes's." NYtimes.com. Accessed December 24, 2016. http://www.nytimes.com/1981/04/19/world/gold-bar-found-in-mexico-thought-to-be-cortes-s.html.

———. "Lost Vivaldi Opera Finally Gets Its Music and Words Together." NYtimes.com. Accessed December 26, 2016. http://www.nytimes.com/2005/06/13/arts/music/lost-vivaldi-opera-finally-gets-its-music-and-words-together.html?_r=0.

Rosenlof, Celeste Tholen. "Filmmakers Search for Montezuma's Treasure in Kanab Pond." Ksl.com. Accessed December 24, 2016. http://www.ksl.com/?nid=1205&sid=28673521.

"The Stolen Treasure of Montezuma." Ancient-origins.net. Accessed December 23, 2016. http://www.ancient-origins.net/myths-legends/stolen-treasure-montezuma-001909.

Voorburg, René. "Introduction to the Aztec Calendar." Azteccalendar.com. Accessed December 17, 2016. https://www.azteccalendar.com/azteccalendar.html.

"What was the Symbol for Gold?" mexicolore.co.uk. Accessed December 26, 2016. http://www.mexicolore.co.uk/aztecs/ask-us/symbol-for-gold.

INDEX

Page numbers in **boldface** are illustrations. Entries in **boldface** are glossary terms.

Anahuac, 11
aqueduct, 24, 47, 91
army, 23, 39–40, 44–45, 47, 54–55, 59, 74–75, 80
astrologer, 16, 45
astronomy, 38, 42–43

brigantine, **83**, 84, 90–92, 94
Burland, Cottie Arthur, 7, 31, 33, 40, 54

calendar, 16, 19–20, 32, 38, 44, 100
calmécac, 23, 35–36, 100
causeway, 21, 64, 73–74, 88, 91–92, 95, 109
central Mexico, 9, 10, 11–12
chinampa, 20
Christianity, 7, 60, 88, 95, 98
City-state, 21
codex, 33, 81, **85**, 100, **101**
codices, 7, 81, 89, 100

conquistador, 6, 33, **50**, 51, **52–53**, 59, 61, 77, 81, 89, 95, 107, 110
Cortés, Hernán, 52–53, 60–61, 62, 63–65, 66, 67–69, 71–75, 77, 80–82, 84, 86–87, 88–89, 90–96, 99, 104, 107, 108, 110
Council of Four, 35, 42, 45, 47, 70–72, 85
Cuauhtémoc, 85, 88–92, 94–95
Cuitláhuac, 70–73, 80, 82, 85

de Aguilar, Gerónimo, 60–61
de Alvarado, Pedro, 69–72
destiny, 28, 32, 51
divinatory, 20
Doña Marina, 61

Eagle Warriors, 41, 54–55, 58, 75
emperor, 5–6, 19–20, 25, 33, 35–36, 39–40, 42–48, 51, 54, 59–60, 65, 67–71, 73, 77, 85, 94–95, 103–106, 112

Index **125**

fate, 12, 27–29, 32, 36, 38, 45–49, 51, 67–70, 104
feathers, 21, 24, 65, 74
festivals, 20, 23, 28, 69, 77
fifth world, 13
friars, 7, 33, 81, 96, 98, 100, 109

Garland Wars, 24
glyph, 16, 109
gods, 5, 11–13, 16, 19–21, 23–25, 27–29, 32, 35–36, 38, 40, 42, 44–49, 51, 59–61, 64–65, 67–70, 80, 84, 88, 94–95, 100, 106–107
gold, 21, 24, 60, 63, 65, 74, 95, 103, 107–110, 108

harquebusier, 56, 70–71
Huitzilopochtli, 8, 11–13, 16, 21, 24, 28, 38, 40, 42, 44, 46, 55, 61, 65, 69

la noche triste/night of sorrows, 7, 74, 77, 80–81, 90, 107
lacustrine, 21
Lake Texcoco, 10, 12, 20, 80, 90, 107–108

magic, 32, 54, 63–64
magic paint, 36, 37, 38

massacre, 70–72, 74
merchants, 21, 25
Mexica, 6, 11, 31, 72
Mexico City, 96, 109–110
military school, 23, 38–39
military technology, 56, 57
Montezuma's Treasure, 108–109

Nahuatl, 6, 9, 48, 60, 96, 100, 107, 110
New Fire Ceremony, 29, 47
New Spain, 33, 81, 95
night journey, 36, 38
nobles, 27–28, 44–46, 54–55, 63, 70

obsidian, 21, 39, 41, 56, 93
ocelot, 40, 54–55, 59, 75
Ocelot Warriors, 40, 41, 54–55, 58, 59, 75
omen, 16, 27, 48, 61

pochtecatl, 25
portent, 16, 27, 51, 61, 104
priests, 5, 16, 18, 23–24, 27, 29, 31–32, 35–36, 38, 42–44, 47, 60, 68, 81, 103
prophecy, 19, 44, 48, 51

Quetzalcoatl, 16, 19, 21,
  32, **34**, 42, 44–45, 48–49,
  59–61, 64–65

rules of warfare, 24, 40, 88

sacrifice, 13, 16, **17**, **18**, 20,
  23–25, 27–29, 38, 40, 42,
  46, 48, 54, 56, 59, 65, 68,
  72, 74, 77, 88, 93
siege, 84, **86–87**, 88, 90–95
signs, 5, 11–12, 16, 27–28,
  35–36, 45–46, 69
slaves, 24, 27, 46
smallpox, 84, 85, 97
subjugation, 47, 89

taxes, 5, 24, 48
telpochcalli, 23, 38–39
temple school, 23, 35–36,
  38–39, 42
Tenochtitlán, **10**, 12, **14–15**,
  20–21, **22**, 23–25, 28, 35,
  40, 46–48, 60–61, 63–64,
  67–69, 71, 73–75, 77, **80**,
  81–82, 84, **86–87**, 88–96,
  100, 107–109
tepuztli, 48
Texcocans, 89, 95
Thomas, Hugh, 7, 31, 100
Tlacaelel, 39–40

Tlaloc, 21, 42, 46, 68
Tlaxcalans, 47–48, 63–64, 69,
  77, 81–82, 90, 93–95
Toltecs, 19, 25, 27, 44–46,
  105, 110
tonalpohualli, 20
tonalpouhque, 16
Totonacs, 61, 63, 65, 84
trade, 25, 45, 89
tribute, 5, 16, 20, 24–25, 28,
  40, 48, 61, 64–65, 68, 82,
  91, 107
Triple Alliance, 21, 24, 28, 89

Vera Cruz, **52–53**, 65, 67, 69,
  84, 93
visions, 48

warrior, 13, 24–25, 35–36,
  38–39, 41–44, **50**, 54–55,
  59, 69–70, 73–75, 90–92,
  94, 103, 109

xiuhpohualli, 19

ABOUT THE AUTHOR

ELIZABETH SCHULZ has a diverse background, having worked in the film and television industry as well as in the private sector. She has been a writer all her life, writing for pleasure as well as projects. A professional proposal writer for business, her creative writing credits include the first thirteen episodes of the WXXI PBS series *New York Wine & Table*, a script commissioned by a performance artist, and story contributions for the daily historical podcast *On This Day Podcast*.